LAW EXPRESS: EQUITY AND TRUSTS

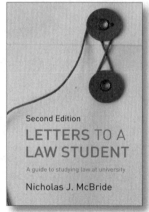

EQUITY AND TRUSTS

3rd edition

John Duddington
Worcester College of Technology

Longman
is an imprint of

Harlow, England • London • New York • Boston • San Francisco • Toronto • Sydney • Singapore • Hong Kong
Tokyo • Seoul • Taipei • New Delhi • Cape Town • Madrid • Mexico City • Amsterdam • Munich • Paris • Milan

Pearson Education Limited
Edinburgh Gate
Harlow
Essex CM20 2JE
England

and Associated Companies throughout the world

Visit us on the World Wide Web at:
www.pearsoned.co.uk

First published 2007
Second edition 2009
Third edition published 2011

© Pearson Education Limited 2007, 2011

ISBN: 978-1-4082-3990-2

British Library Cataloguing-in-Publication Data
A catalogue record for this book is available from the British Library

Library of Congress Cataloging-in-Publication Data
Duddington, John.
   Equity and trusts / John Duddington. – 3rd ed.
      p. cm.
   Includes index.
   ISBN 978-1-4082-3990-2 (pbk.)
   1. Equity–England–Outlines, syllabi, etc. 2. Trusts and trustees–England–Outlines, syllabi, etc.
I. Title.
   KD674.D83 2010
   346.4205'9–dc22

                                                                        2010019033

10 9 8 7 6 5 4 3 2 1
13 12 11 10

Typeset in 10pt Helvetica Condensed by 3
Printed by Ashford Colour Press Ltd., Gosport

Contents

Acknowledgements   vii
Introduction   ix
Guided tour   xii
Guided tour of the companion website   xiv
Table of cases and statutes   xvi

Chapter 1: Nature of equity and trusts   1
Chapter 2: Equitable remedies and doctrines   15
Chapter 3: The three certainties   33
Chapter 4: The beneficiary principle and purpose trusts 49
Chapter 5: Formalities   65
Chapter 6: Constitution   83
Chapter 7: Secret and half-secret trusts   101
Chapter 8: Resulting trusts   117
Chapter 9: Constructive trusts and estoppel   131
Chapter 10: Charitable trusts   149
Chapter 11: Trusteeship   171
Chapter 12: Breach of trust   187

And finally, before the exam ...   203

Glossary of terms   207
Index   210

Supporting resources

Visit the Law Express series companion website at **www.pearsoned.co.uk/ lawexpress** to find valuable student learning material including:

- A study plan test to assess how well you know the subject before you begin your revision, now broken down into targeted study units
- Interactive quizzes with a variety of question types to test your knowledge of the main points from each chapter of the book
- Further examination questions and guidelines for answering them
- Interactive flashcards to help you revise the main terms and cases
- Printable versions of the topic maps and checklists
- 'You be the marker' allows you to see exam questions and answers from the perspective of the examiner and includes notes on how an answer might be marked
- Podcasts provide point-by-point instruction on how to answer a common exam question

Also: The companion website provides the following features:

- Search tool to help locate specific items of content
- E-mail results and profile tools to send results of quizzes to instructors
- Online help and support to assist with website usage and troubleshooting

For more information please contact your local Pearson Education sales representative or visit **www.pearsoned.co.uk/lawexpress**.

Acknowledgements

To my father, Walter Duddington, who first encouraged me to become a lawyer, and who would, I am sure, have been an equity enthusiast; to my wife Anne, for her constant support, loyalty and technical expertise without which my books would never begin to be written; to my daughter Mary, for her seemingly faultless proofreading and sense of fun which keeps me going; and to my son Christopher for just being himself. I would also like to thank my colleagues at Worcester Law School in the Property Law Team, Deborah Lister, Fiona ShawRoberts and Lesley Smallman, who have contributed more than they know!

Nor must I forget the staff of Pearson Education, especially Zoë Botterill and Christine Statham, for their endless encouragement, cheerfulness and practical guidance, and the reviewers who sent in such detailed and helpful suggestions for this edition. I would have been delighted to have adopted more of these but for the limitations of space. However, I do hope that they see at least some of their ideas reflected in the pages of this book.

Finally aficionados of this book may see that for this edition I have expanded Chapter 9 by the addition of new material on estoppel in view of the recent activities of the courts in this area which make it a likely subject for exam questions. This has meant that variation of trusts no longer has a separate chapter of its own but the material on this topic has found a happy home in Chapter 11.

John Duddington
January 2010

Publisher's acknowledgements

Our thanks go to all reviewers who contributed to the development of this text, including students who participated in research and focus groups which helped to shape the series format.

Introduction

Most students achieve an average mark in equity exams, some do not pass at all, and others do very well. So far this is typical of all exams, but in my experience the number of students who do very well is smaller than in other law exams. Why? This introduction aims to give you some pointers to getting into the category of those who do very well, and equally pointers for simply achieving a pass.

What are the problems which students commonly face in tackling these questions?

■ Essay questions

Equity is founded on a number of doctrines such as the concept of a fiduciary, unconscionability, notice and discretion in the grant of remedies. Students often simply scratch the surface when discussing these and this is the major reason why they do essay questions badly.

Take the concept of a fiduciary.

This is relevant in questions on constructive trusts, trustees, the nature of equity and undue influence. As such it is very well worth knowing some ideas of precisely what it means. But take a typical answer to this question:

'The concept of a fiduciary is at the heart of equity.' What do you understand by the term 'fiduciary' and to what extent is this true?

This appears to be relatively easy. Students can remember cases in which the fiduciary concept has been relevant and they put them together. I have read hundreds of answers like this. Cases such as *Boardman* v *Phipps* (1967) and *A-G for Hong Kong* v *Reid* (1994) are dealt with and in each instance it is remarked that they are instances of the fiduciary principle. Possibly *Queensland Mines Ltd* v *Hudson* is mentioned as an example of where the fiduciary principle did not apply.

This is leading to a mark of around 50 per cent. There is knowledge of the case law and students will be surprised that they have not done better in spite of all their work. The reason is simple: they have just scratched the surface. No attempt has been made to deal with the nature of the fiduciary concept. What is it about? A good answer would explain that the central idea is that of loyalty, which then translates into a principle that the fiduciary must not allow a conflict of interest between their duties as a fiduciary and their personal interests. How do fiduciary relationships arise? Is it through a voluntary undertaking on the part of the fiduciary? Moreover, the above examples of fiduciary relationships only refer to trustees. What about undue influence? Remember to take examples from as wide an area as possible. (Fiduciaries are mainly dealt with in Chapter 9 (for constructive trusts) and Chapter 2 (for undue influence).) We will return to this question in the conclusion.

A student intervenes at this point.

How can I cover all the cases *and* deal with the theoretical issues?

Answer: you cannot so you will not be penalised for not doing so. Select a few cases, learn them well, read around them and relate them to the theoretical issues you have discussed. You will now be on the way to a good pass. *Less detail – more depth.*

◼ Problem questions

These are easier as the structure of the problem gives you the structure of your answer. However, in equity problems there are often rather subtle points which, when picked up, can give you extra marks. A good example is secret and half-secret trusts (see Chapter 7), a very common area for problems.

Here is one example:

The generally accepted rule for communication of a half-secret trust is that the details of the trust must be communicated before the will (*Re Keen* (1937)). However, *Re Keen* is also authority for another rule which can conflict with this: that the details must be communicated in accordance with the terms of the will. Again an answer which scores about 50 per cent will mention and apply the first rule, which is probably the correct one. However, an answer which also applies the other rule will clearly score more. (These rules are all dealt with in Chapter 7.) Another subtle point arising here is the law where the trust is communicated to one trustee but not the other. Is the one to whom it is not communicated bound? (See *Re Stead* (1900).) Learn these rather tricky points thoroughly! Constitution of trusts is another area with many a subtlety!

◼ About this book

This book is not a potted version of the subject. You will not find in it all the detail which you need to pass your exams. It is an aid to learning and not a substitute to reading textbooks, articles (essential if you want a good pass) and of course attendance at lectures, tutorials and seminars. It can be used either at the end of the course as a revision aid or during the course to guide you along.

REVISION NOTE

Success in exams in equity and trusts requires the following:

- An ability to tackle essay questions in such areas as the nature of equity, constructive trusts and equitable remedies
- An ability to tackle complex problem questions in areas such as constitution of trusts, charities and secret trusts
- Dealing with theoretical concepts (usually at the start of your answer)
- Using a wide range of examples.

Before you begin, you can use the study plan available on the companion website to assess how well you know the material in this book and identify the areas where you may want to focus your revision.

Guided tour

Topic maps – Visual guides highlight key subject areas and facilitate easy navigation through the chapter. Download them from the companion website to pin to your wall or add to your own revision notes.

Revision checklists – How well do you know each topic? Use these to identify essential points you should know for your exams. But don't panic if you don't know them all – the chapters will help you revise each point to ensure you are fully prepared for your exams. Print the checklists off the companion website and track your revision progress!

Revision checklist

Essential points you should

- [ ] the characteristics of equitable
- [ ] the situations in which a grant performance, rescission and r
- [ ] the meaning of undue influe
- [ ] the situations when undu
- [ ] the effect of undue in

Sample questions – Practice makes perfect! Read the question at the start of each chapter and consider how you would answer it. Guidance on structuring strong answers is provided at the end of the chapter. Try out additional sample questions online.

Sample question

Could you answer this question? Below is a typical essay question that could arise on this topic. Guidelines on answering the question are included at the end of this chapter, while a sample problem question and guidance on tackling it can be found on the companion website.

Assessment advice – Not sure how best to tackle a problem or essay question? Wondering what you may be asked? Be prepared – use the assessment advice to identify the ways in which a subject may be examined and how to apply your knowledge effectively.

ASSESSMENT ADVICE

Essay questions An essay will often deal with equitable remedies and may ask you to consider them in the light of a particular quotation. This should not pose great problems of understanding; rather the problem is often the amount of material to hand and the consequent danger of simply ploughing through it with no real attempt to answer the question. The golden rule applies: make a selection of material and then use it to address the issues raised in the question. Nothing more! Other possibilities are essays on undue influence, especially the decision in *Barclays Bank* v *O'Brien* (1994), and on the developing case law on breach of confidence.

Don't be tempted to... – Underline areas where students most often trip up in exams. Use them to avoid making common mistakes and losing marks.

! Don't be tempted to...

Make sure that, having first decided that this is a possible undue influence case, you then move on immediately to see where in the above categories it falls. This will decide the rest of the case as it is vital to know if undue influence has to be proved or not.

Make your answer stand out – Illustrates sources of further thinking and debate where you can maximise your marks. Use these to really impress your examiners!

TABLE REMEDIES A

✓ Make your answer

Search orders were criticised o
conduct, amounting to the rans
proved against that person. S
ample, *Lock International*

> **KEY CASE**
>
> *Sky Petroleum v VIP Petroleum* [1974] 1 WLR 576
> *Concerning: grant of an injunction, which would amount to specific performance, where damages would not be an adequate remedy*
>
> **Facts**
> During a petrol shortage the defendants terminated their contract with the claimants to supply them with petrol.
>
> **Legal principle**
> An injunction was granted restraining the defendants from withholding supplies of petrol. There was a petrol shortage at the time and so, if only damages had been awarded to the claimants, they would have been unlikely to obtain supplies elsewhere.

Key cases and key statutes – Identify the important elements of the essential cases and statutes you will need to know for your exams.

> **KEY STATUTE**
>
> **Trade Union and Labour Relations Act 1992, s. 236**
> This prohibits the courts from enforcing performance of contracts of employment either by specific performance or injunction. This only applies to actual contracts of employment, not to other contracts of personal service. See *Page One Records v Britton (t/a The Troggs)* [1967] and *Warren v Mendy* (1989).

Key definitions – Make sure you understand essential legal terms. Use the flashcards online to test your recall!

> **KEY DEFINITION: Rectification**
>
> Where a written instrument (e.g. a contract) does not accord with the actual intentions of the parties it can be made to do so by an order of rectification.

Glossary – Forgotten the meaning of a word? This quick reference covers key definitions and other useful terms.

Glossary of terms

The glossary is divided into two parts: *key definitions* and *other useful terms*. The key definitions can be found within the chapter in which they occur, as well as here, below. These definitions are the essential terms that you must know and understand in order to prepare for an exam. The additional list of terms provides further definitions of useful terms and phrases which will also help you answer examination and coursework questions effectively. These terms are highlighted in the text as they occur but the definition can only be found here.

Exam tips – Feeling the pressure? These boxes indicate how you can improve your exam performance and your chances of getting those top marks!

> **EXAM TIP**
>
> Freezing, and especially search orders, are an area where there is room for debate about the need to consider the interests of the party seeking the order and the party against whom it is being sought. Think about this issue for an essay question.

Revision notes – Highlight related points or areas of overlap in other topics, or areas where your course might adopt a particular approach that you should check with your course tutor.

> **REVISION NOTE**
>
> Go back to Chapter 1 and check that you are familiar with this case. It is an excellent illustration of equitable remedies.

Guided tour of the companion website

Book resources are available to download. Print your own **topic maps** and **revision checklists**!

Use the **study plan** prior to your revision to help you assess how well you know the subject and determine which areas need most attention. Choose to take the full assessment or focus on targeted study units.

'**Test your knowledge**' of individual areas with quizzes tailored specifically to each chapter. **Sample problem and essay questions** are also available with guidance on crafting a good answer.

Flashcards help improve recall of important legal terms and key cases and statutes. Available in both electronic and printable formats.

'You be the marker' gives you the chance to evaluate sample exam answers for different question types and understand how and why an examiner awards marks.

Download the podcast and listen as your own personal Law Express tutor guides you through a 10–15 minute audio session. You will be presented with a typical but challenging question and provided a step-by-step explanation on how to approach the question, what essential elements your answer will need for a pass, how to structure a good response, and what to do to make your answer stand out so that you can earn extra marks.

All of this and more can be found when you visit www.pearsoned.co.uk/lawexpress

Table of cases and statutes

Cases

Abacus Trust Co. (Isle of Man) Ltd. v NSPCC (2001) STC 1344 177

Abou-Rahmah v Abacha (2006) EWCA Civ. 1492 196

American Cyanamid Co. v Ethicon Ltd [1975] 2 WLR 396, [1975] AC 396 HL 20

Anthony v Donges (1998) 2 FLR 775 HC 39

Anton Piller KG v Manufacturing Processes Ltd [1976] Ch 55 7, 21

Armitage v Nurse [1998] Ch 221 HC 181

Attorney General for Hong Kong v Reid [1994] AC 324 HL 138, 190

Australian Securities and Investments Commission v Citigroup Global Markets Australia Pty Ltd (2007) FCA 963 182

Barclays Bank Ltd v Quistclose Investments Ltd [1970] AC 567 HL 8, 119, 122, 125, 126, 127

Barclays Bank plc v O'Brien [1994] 1 AC 180 17, 28, 29

Barlow Clowes International Ltd (in liquidation) v Eurotrust International Ltd (2006) 1 WLR 1476 195, 196

Barlow Clowes International Ltd (in liquidation) v Vaughan [1992] 4 All ER 22 200, 201

Bank of Credit and Commerce International (Overseas) Ltd (in liquidation) v Akindele [2001] Ch 437 194

Binions v Evans [1972] Ch 359 133, 141

Bishopsgate Investment Management (in liquidation) v Homan [1995] Ch 211 CA 197

Blackwell v Blackwell [1929] AC 318 105, 106

Boardman v Phipps [1967] 2 AC 46 HL 12, 133, 136, 137, 142, 145, 173, 174, 184, 193

Bray v Ford [1896] AC 44 135

Bristol and West Building Society v Mothew (1998) Ch 1 137

Burns v Burns [1984] 1 All ER 244 140

Cannon v Hartley [1949] Ch 213 92

Carly v Farrelly (1975) 1 NZLR 356 141

Carreras Rothmans Ltd v Freeman Matthews Treasure Ltd (1985) Ch 207 127

Charter plc v City Index Ltd and others (2007) EWCA Civ. 1382 194

Chichester Diocesan Fund and Board of Finance Inc. v Simpson [1944] AC 341 HL 162–3, 167

Choithram (T) International SA v Pagarani [2001] 2 All ER 492 PC 85, 89, 92, 98

Church of Scientology v Kaufman [1973] RFC 635 156, 157

Citibank NA v MIBA Assurance SA (2006) EWHC 3215 182

Clayton's Case *see Re* Clayton

Comiskey v Bowring-Hanbury [1905] AC 84 HL 37–8

Co-operative Insurance Society Ltd v Argyll Stores (Holdings) Ltd [1998] AC 1 HL 24

Cowan v Scargill [1985] Ch 270 179

Craddock Bros v Hunt [1923] 2 Ch 136 HC 26

Curtis v Rippon (1820) 5 Madd 434 HC 40, 41

Dillwyn v Llewellyn (1862) 4 de GF and J 517 97

Dingle v Turner [1972] 1 All ER 878 HL 159

Duggan v Governor of Full Sutton Prison (2004) 2 All ER 966 38

Dunbar Bank plc v Nadeem (1997) 2 All ER 253 29

Dyer v Dyer (1788) 30 ER 42 123

Ellison v Ellison (1802) 6 Ves 656 87

Eves v Eves [1975] 3 All ER 768 140, 141

Farah Constructions Pty Ltd and others v Say-Dee Pty Ltd (2007) HCA 22 141, 194, 195

Foskett v McKeown [2001] 1 AC 102 HL 197, 199, 201

Gardner v Rowe (1828) 5 Russ 258 69

Gilmour v Coates [1949] AC 426 HL 11, 54, 161

Goodchild v Bradbury (2006) EWCA Civ. 1868 27

Gold v Hill (1998) Fam Law 664 107

Grey v IRC [1960] AC 1 HL 73, 80

Halifax Building Society v Thomas (1995) 4 All ER 673 141

Hill v CA Parsons and Co. Ltd [1972] Ch 305 25

Hodgson v Marks (1971) 1 Ch 892 70, 123

Holder v Holder [1968] Ch 353 176

Howe v Earl of Dartmouth (1802) 7 Ves 137 Chan 177

Hubbard v Pitt [1976] QB 142 20

Hunter v Moss [1994] 3 All ER 40

Hussey v Palmer (1972) 3 All ER 744 141

IRC v Broadway Cottages Trust [1955] Ch 20 42

Jones v Lock (1865) 1 Ch App 25 89

Keech v Sandford (1726) Sel Cas Ch 61 Ct of Chan 136, 145, 173

Klug v Klug (1918) 2 Ch 67 176

Knight v Knight (1840) 3 Beav 148 36

Laskar v Laskar (2008) All ER (D) 104 123, 140

Leahy v A-G for New South Wales [1959] AC 457 54

Lloyds Bank plc v Rosset [1991] 1 AC 107 140

Lock International plc v Beswick (1989) 3 All ER 373 22

Mareva Compania Naviera SA v International Bulk Carriers SA (The Mareva) [1980] 1 All ER 213 7, 21

Mascall v Mascall (1985) P & CR 119 91

McCormick v Grogan (1869) LR 4 HL 82 106

McGovern v Attorney-General [1981] 3 All ER 493 HC 162

McPhail v Doulton [1971] AC 424 HL 35, 42, 45, 47, 115, 153

Midland Bank Trust Co. Ltd v Green [1981] AC 513 HL 139

Milroy v Lord (1862) 4 De GF & J 264 88

Morice v Bishop of Durham (1805) 10 Ves 522 35, 53

Moss v Cooper (1861) 1 John & H 352 108, 115

Motivex Ltd v Bulfield [1988] 2 BCLC 104 135

Mussett v Bingle [1876] WN 170 56

Neville v Wilson [1997] Ch 144 75

Oppenheim v Tobacco Securities Trust Co. Ltd [1951] AC 297 HL 11, 160, 167, 168

Ottaway v Norman [1972] Ch 698 107

Oughtred v IRC [1960] AC 206 HL 67, 75, 76

Page One Records Ltd v Britton (t/a The Troggs) [1967] 3 All ER 822 HC 91

Palmer v Simmonds (1854) 2 Drew 221 39

Patel v Ali [1984] Ch 283 HC 5, 6, 18, 31

Pallant v Morgan [1952] Ch 43 138

Paul v Constance [1977] 1 All ER 195 38, 89

Pecore v Pecore (2007) 1 SCR 795 123

Pennington v Waine [2002] EWCA Civ 227, [2002] 1 WLR 2075 CA 4, 11, 85, 91, 98

Pullan v Koe [1913] 1 Ch 9 92

Queensland Mines Ltd v Hudson (1978) 18 ALR 1 PC 11, 137, 145

R. v Clowes (No. 2) [1994] 2 All ER 316 38

R. v District Auditor, ex parte West Yorkshire MCC [1986] RVR 24 44

Re Abbott (1982) 3 All ER 181 125

Re Adams and Kensington Vestry (1884) 27 Ch D 394 CA 37, 38, 47

Re Astor's Settlement Trusts [1952] Ch 534 HC 52, 53, 54

Re Baden's Deed Trusts (No. 2) [1973] Ch 9 43

Re Barlow's Will Trusts (1979) 1 WLR 278 HC 45, 47

Re Beloved Wilkes' Charity (1851) 3 Mac & G 540 HC 176

Re Boyes (1884) 26 Ch D 531 108

Re Bucks Constabulary Widows' and Orphans' Fund Friendly Society (No. 2) (1979) 1 WLR 396 166

Re CL [1969] 1 Ch 587 Court of Protection 183

Re Clayton (1816) 1 Mer 572 199–200, 201

Re Cooper (Colin) [1939] Ch 811 112

Re Compton (1945) 1 All ER 198 158

Re Cook's Settlement Trusts [1965] Ch 902 94

Re Coulthurst [1951] Ch 661 HC 155

Re Craig (1971) Ch 95 26

Re Danish Bacon Co. Ltd Staff Pension Fund [1971] 1 WLR 248 HC 78

Re Dean (1889) 41 Ch Div 552 55

Re Denley's Trust Deed [1969] 1 Ch 373 HC 55, 56, 61

Re Diggles (1888) 39 Ch Div 253 37

Re Diplock [1948] Ch 465 197, 201

Re Endacott [1960] Ch 232 54, 55

Re Faraker [1912] 2 Ch 488 165

Re Farepak Food and Gifts Ltd (in administration) (2006) EWHC 3272 HC 38, 126, 127, 141

Re Finger's Will Trusts [1972] Ch 286 165

Re Gardner [1920] 2 Ch 523 112, 115

Re Gillingham Bus Disaster Fund [1959] Ch 62 125, 166

Re Golay [1965] 1 WLR 969 47

Re Goldcorp Exchange Ltd (in receivership) [1995] 1 AC 74 40

Re Gonin [1979] Ch16 96

Re Grant's Will Trusts [1979] 3 All ER 359 HC 54, 60, 61

Re Haines (1952) The Times 7 November 1952 56

Re Hallett's Estate (1880) 13 Ch D 696 HC 198, 201

Re Harding (2007) EWHC 3 HC 38

Re Harwood [1936] Ch 285 164

Re Hastings-Bass (1975) Ch 25 176

Re Hay's Settlement Trusts [1982] 1 WLR 202 43, 75

Re Hooper [1932] 1 Ch 38 **55, 57**

Re Hopkins' Will Trusts [1965] Ch 669 HC **155–6**

Re Horley Town Football Club; Hunt *v* McLaren (2006) EWHC 2386 HC **59, 60**

Re Jones [1953] Ch 125 **44**

Re Kay [1939] Ch 329 **94**

Re Keen [1937] Ch 236 CA **103, 108, 109, 110, 115**

Re Kershaw's Trusts (1868) LR 6 Eq 322 HC **179**

Re Koettgen's Will Trusts [1954] Ch 252 HC **160, 167**

Re Lipinski's Will Trusts (1976) Ch 235 **59, 61**

Re London Wine Co. (Shippers) Ltd [1986] PCC 121 HC **35, 40**

Re Londonderry's Settlement [1965] Ch 518 **177**

Re Niyazi's Will Trusts [1978] 3 All ER 785 HC **155**

Re Oatway [1903] 2 Ch 356 **198, 201**

Re Osaba (1979) 1 WLR 247 **125**

Re Paradise Motor Co. Ltd [1968] 1 WLR 1125 HC **77**

Re Polly Peck International plc (No. 2) (1998) 3 All ER 812 **141**

Re Pryce [1917] 1 Ch 234 **94**

Re Ralli's Will Trust [1964] Ch 288 HC **95**

Re Recher's Will Trusts [1972] Ch 526 HC **58, 59, 61**

Re Rees [1950] Ch 204 **112, 115**

Re Remnant's Settlement Trusts [1970] Ch 560 HC **183**

Re Rose [1952] Ch 499 HC **91, 98**

Re Rymer [1895] 1Ch19 **165**

Re Slevin [1891] 2 Ch 236 **165**

Re Stead [1900] 1 Ch 237 HC **103, 111**

Re Tilley's Will Trust [1967] Ch 1179 **201**

Re Tuck's Settlement Trusts [1978] Ch 49 HC **44**

Re Tyler's Fund Trusts [1967] 1 WLR 1269 **71, 112, 115**

Re Vandervell's Trusts (No. 2) [1974] Ch 269 CA **74, 121, 128**

Re Vinogradoff [1935] WN 68 **122**

Re West Sussex Constabulary's Widows, Children and Benevolent Fund Trusts [1970] 1 All ER 544 **166**

Re Weston's Settlements [1969] 1 Ch 233 CA **183**

Re Young [1951] Ch 344 **112**

Regal (Hastings) Ltd *v* Gulliver (1942) 1 All ER 378 **137**

Richards *v* Delbridge (1874) LR 18 Eq 11 **89, 98**

Rochefoucauld *v* Boustead [1897] 1 Ch 196 CA **69, 138**

Roscoe (James) (Bolton) *v* Winder [1915] 1 Ch 62 **198, 201**

Royal Bank of Scotland *v* Etridge (No. 2) [2001] UKHL 44 HL, [2002] 2 AC 773 **27, 28, 29**

Saunders *v* Vautier (1841) Cr & Ph 240 CA **182**

Sen *v* Hedley [1991] Ch 425 CA **96–7, 98**

Schmidt *v* Rosewood Trust Ltd (2003) 2 WLR 1442 **177**

Shaw *v* Finnemore (2009) EWHC 367 **27**

Sieff *v* Fox (2005) EWHC 1312 **176, 177**

Sky Petroleum *v* VIP Petroleum Ltd [1974] 1 WLR 576 **23**

Stack *v* Dowden (2007) UKHL 17 **123, 140, 141**

Strong *v* Bird (1874) LR 18 Eq 315 CA **95–6, 98**

Tang Man Sit *v* Capacious Investments Ltd [1996] 1 All ER 193 **193**

Target Holdings Ltd *v* Redferns (a firm) [1996] 1 AC 421 HL **189, 193**

Tempest v Lord Camoys (1882) 21 Ch D 571 176
Templeton Insurance Ltd. v Penningtons (2006) EWHC 685 126
Thorner v Major (2009) UKHL 18 141, 144
Thornton v Howe (1862) 31 Beav 14 Ct of Chan 156
Tinker v Tinker [1970] 2 WLR 331 124
Tinsley v Milligan [1992] Ch 310 CA; [1994] 1 AC340 HL 7, 124
Torquay Hotel Co. Ltd v Cousins [1969] 1 All ER 522 19
TSB v Camfield (1995) 1 All ER 951 29
Twinsectra Ltd v Yardley [2002] 2 AC 164 194, 195, 196
United Scientific Holdings v Burnley BC [1978] AC 904 9
Universal Thermosensors Ltd v Hibben [1992] 1 WLR 840 22
Vandervell v IRC [1967] 2 AC 291 HL 67, 74, 77
Wallbank and Wallbank v Price (2008) 2 FLR 501 38
Wallgrave v Tebbs (1855) 2 K & J 313 HC 108
Walsh v Lonsdale (1882) 21 Ch D 9 HC 10
Warner Bros Pictures Inc. v Nelson [1937] 1 KB 209 HC 25
Warren v Mendy [1989] 3 All ER 103 24
Westdeutsche Landesbank Girozentrale v Islington LBC [1996] AC 669 121
Woodford v Smith [1970] 1 WLR 806 19
Yeoman's Row Management Ltd v Cobbe [2008] UKHL 55 134, 142, 143, 144

Statutes

Charities Act 1993
s. 13 165

Charities Act 2006 58, 151, 156–9
s. 2(2) 154
s. 2(2)(a) 155
s. 2(2)(b) 155–6
s. 2(2)(c) 156
s. 2(2)(d)–(j) 157
s. 2(2)(k) 157
s. 2(2)(l)–(m) 157
s. 3(2) 158
s. 3(3) 158
s. 4(1) 158
s. 14 166
Companies Act 2006
s. 175 137
s. 175(4)(b) 137
Contracts (Rights of Third Parties) Act 1999 91, 94
s. 1 94
s. 7(3) 94
European Convention on Human Rights 156
Art. 5, Protocol 7 123
Family Law Act 1996 19
Family Law (Scotland) Act 2006 141
Judicature Act 1873 9–10
s. 25(11) 9, 10
Judicature Act 1875 9–10
Land Charges Act 1972 139
Law of Property Act 1925 80
s. 52(1) 90, 98
s. 53(1)(b) 68, 69–70, 71, 76, 80, 90, 113, 115, 120
s. 53(1)(c) 70, 71–2, 73, 74, 75, 78, 80, 82, 120
s. 53(2) 69, 70, 71, 113, 120
s. 175 180
Perpetuities and Accumulations Act 1964
s. 5A 56
s. 15(4) 56
Perpetuities and Accumulations Act 2009 61
s. 5 56

s. 7 56
s. 16 56
Recreational Charities Act 1958 158
Statute of Charitable Uses Act 1601 151
Trade Union and Labour Relations Act
  1992
s. 236 24
Trustee Act 1925 173
  s. 31 180, 184
  s. 32 184
  s. 36(1) 175
  s. 39 175
  s. 41 175
  s. 57 182

s. 61 200
s. 62 200
s. 69(2) 177
Trustee Act 2000 173, 174, 178
  s. 1 178, 181, 182
  s. 3 178, 181, 182
  s. 4 178, 182
  s. 5 179
  s. 8 180
  s. 11 181, 182
  s. 29 176
Variation of Trusts Act 1958 182
Wills Act 1837 103

Nature of equity and trusts

1

Revision checklist

Essential points you should know:

- [ ] the meanings of the term equity
- [ ] the reasons why equity developed as a separate system of law
- [ ] what is meant by the concept of a trust
- [ ] the later development of equity in outline
- [ ] the modern arguments for and against whether equity and the common law are now fused

■Topic map

Meaning of equity

Historical development
of equity – contrast
with common law

Judicature Acts 1873
to 1875.
Question of fusion

Modern equity:
development since 1873

◼Introduction

This chapter is perhaps the most important in this book.

However, unlike all others chapters, it does not contain all the material needed to answer a question.

The reason is that this chapter sets the scene for a study of equity and, in addition to guiding you on the meaning of the term 'equity' and the history of its development, it points you in the direction of various themes in the study of equity. The detail on some of these will be found in later chapters. A question on the nature and/or development of equity will obviously be an essay one. This is one area where it is absolutely essential to read beyond the standard textbooks in order to gain an above average pass on a question and this chapter points you in the direction of a variety of additional reading in the 'Make your answer stand out' sections.

It also has a separate section on the development of the trust and the uses to which trusts can be put today. This often forms the subject of an exam question and, again, this section points you in the direction of themes which are picked up in more depth in later chapters.

ASSESSMENT ADVICE

An essay question can take one of these forms:

- The historical development of equity. This would be less likely than the other possibilities.
- The relationship between equity and the common law. This is the most likely area, as it will involve you in looking at the distinctive features of equity and contrasting them with the common law. There is the opportunity to use your knowledge of other areas (e.g. contract and tort) when you discuss the common law and this will gain added marks.
- The possibility of equity and the common law converging in the future. This is an area on which a good deal has been written recently and so you need to have read widely in order to be able to answer it well. On the whole it is not dealt with in much depth in the standard textbooks.
- The uses to which trusts can be put with an emphasis on their versatility.

▶

Two other points:

■ It is possible for a question to cover all of these issues, for example, it may ask you to analyse the reasons why equity developed, how significant it is today and how it may develop in future.

■ Be careful to check whether the question asks you to discuss 'modern equity'. Modern really means since the Judicature Acts and so no credit will be given for historical material here. It is a common error among students to feel that they must include historical material whatever the question says. Resist it!

■ Sample question

Could you answer this question? Below is a typical essay question that could arise on this topic. Guidelines on answering the question are included at the end of this chapter, while another sample essay question and guidance on tackling it can be found on the companion website.

ESSAY QUESTION

'The courts in their equitable jurisdiction have more scope for developing the law in a conscionable manner than they have in their common law jurisdiction.'

(Hayton and Marshall, 2005)

Evaluate this statement by reference to the growth and development of modern equity.

■ Meaning of equity

Equity has various meanings. In a general sense equity means fairness or justice. However, this is too general on its own for law exams and also it takes us into a wider debate about what precisely 'fairness' and 'justice' mean. Instead we need to:

■ consider the term 'conscience': this has a long history in equity – the Chancellor was known as the Keeper of the King's Conscience

■ consider recent cases where the courts have used the term 'unconscionability' which at least is derived from conscience (e.g. see *Pennington* v *Waine* (2002) in Chapter 6)

- make it clear that equity today does not mean the same as justice in the broad sense

- contrast equity with other terms (e.g. charity and mercy)

- state the principle that equity may intervene where the application of a strict rule of law would cause injustice (e.g. it might allow a mortgage to be redeemed even though the actual redemption date had passed)

- state that in the legal sense equity means the body of principles developed by the Court of Chancery.

 Make your answer stand out

You will certainly improve your mark in an essay question on the nature of equity if you read beyond the standard textbooks in this area. A good place to start is Watt (2009) especially pages 36–41 on 'Multiple Meanings of Equity'. Even better would be to read (or see!) Shakespeare's *Measure for Measure* which has a lot to say on these themes.

In an essay on the nature of equity you could then move on to look at characteristics of equity: it is discretionary, it acts as a supplement to the common law (not a complete system on its own), it acts *in personam*, etc.

For all these points you need examples drawn from equity and this is a good opportunity to show your wide knowledge.

KEY CASE

Patel v *Ali* (1984) Ch. 283 (HC)

Concerning: principles for the grant of an equitable remedy

Facts

A contract was made for the sale of a house but during a long delay in going on to completion the seller had a leg amputated and she gave birth to her second and third children. This meant that she came to rely on help from friends and relatives. The buyers sought **specific performance** (SP) (equitable remedy) to compel the seller to complete.

Legal principle

SP would be refused as there would be hardship amounting to injustice if it was granted because the seller would lose the help on which she relied if she was forced to move.

Patel v *Ali* is an excellent case to build part of an answer on the nature of equity round. It shows:

- Equitable remedies are discretionary – common law ones are not. She would have to pay damages (common law remedy) for her breach of the contract of sale.

- Equity is not just a question of the court exercising a complete discretion: there are certain principles on which it exercises a discretion. In the above case the court emphasised that to compel the seller to move would amount to 'hardship amounting to injustice'. The normal rule is that SP is granted in contracts for the sale of land where the seller fails to complete; in this case the rule was displaced. An exam question often asks if equity is just a matter of the court in each case having a complete discretion. Here is part of your answer, although you will need to say that some judges do give the impression that equity is just individual discretion on their part – see below.

 Make your answer stand out

You should research the term 'unconscionability'. Take this quote from Duddington (2006: 18): 'unconscionability is valuable as a general pointer to the direction to which equity should take, but it is of no use as a practical tool in the application of equitable principles, for, in the end, principle is what equity is about.' Note the mention of equity being based on principle and link this to the discussion of discretion in equity below. Read Hopkins (2006) who considers the utility of unconscionability as a rationale for equitable intervention.

Figure 1.1

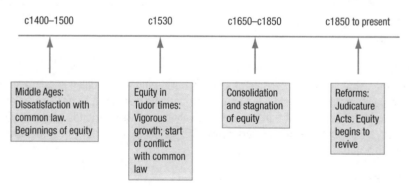

c1400–1500	c1530	c1650–c1850	c1850 to present
Middle Ages: Dissatisfaction with common law. Beginnings of equity	Equity in Tudor times: Vigorous growth; start of conflict with common law	Consolidation and stagnation of equity	Reforms: Judicature Acts. Equity begins to revive

Exam questions are not likely to ask you just for an historical account of equity and so you should look at the history to see if it gives pointers to how equity operates today, which is a much more likely area for a question.

▉ Maxims of equity

These are signposts to how equitable jurisdiction might be exercised but not fixed rules. Examples (and where illustrations on their application may be found in this book) are:

- Equity looks to the intent and not the form (Chapters 6 and 7)
- Equity will not allow a statute to be used as an instrument of fraud (Chapters 7 and 9)
- Equity will not assist a **volunteer** (Chapter 6).

KEY DEFINITION: Volunteer

A person who has not provided any consideration for a promise.

Look at how equity developed as a supplement to the common law (e.g. by using remedies such as **injunctions** and SP to prevent injustice and then mention that this is still the case today (e.g. the modern *Mareva* (freezing) and *Anton Piller* (search) orders which are examples of injunctions (see Chapter 2)).

KEY DEFINITION: Injunction

An order requiring a party either to do or not to do a particular act.

Look at how equity gradually developed maxims and then give examples of how these are still used today.

 Make your answer stand out

Tinsley v *Milligan* (1994) is an excellent example of how the Court of Appeal and the House of Lords both used the maxim 'he who comes to equity must come with clean hands' but applied it differently (see Chapter 8).

You should also look at how trusts were originally used and at how the trust concept has developed today.

■ Development of the trust

You may not get questions on the historical development of the trust but you should use this chapter to make sure that you are absolutely clear on the following fundamental points.

What is a trust?

> **KEY DEFINITION: Trust**
>
> This is a relationship which arises when property is vested in a person (or persons) called the trustees, which those trustees are obliged to hold for the benefit of other persons called the cestuis que trust or beneficiaries' (Hanbury and Martin (2009): 49).

Who is the settlor?

> **KEY DEFINITION: Settlor**
>
> The creator of the trust which is created by the settlor transferring property to the trustees to hold on trust or alternatively declaring that they are the trustees. If the trust is created by will then the trust is created by the testator.

Who are the beneficiaries?

> **KEY DEFINITION: Beneficiaries**
>
> Those for whom the property is held on trust and therefore they have the equitable interest in the property.

The idea that the **beneficiaries** have an equitable interest in the **trust** property is one of the concepts at the heart of equity. It underlies cases such as *Barclays Bank* v *Quistclose Investments Ltd* (1970) (see Chapter 8). The effect is that in equity the beneficiaries own the trust property and so if it is wrongly taken from the trust they are not just in the position of creditors who have to claim the return of money owed to them as a debt. Instead the beneficiaries may be able to use the remedies set out in Chapter 12.

Suppose that someone has purchased the trust property. Can the beneficiaries reclaim it from them? This brings us to another definition.

KEY DEFINITION: Notice

A purchaser has notice of an equitable interest and so is bound by it unless they had either actual notice of the equitable interest of the beneficiaries, or constructive notice or imputed notice.

- Actual notice means actual knowledge
- Constructive notice means that the purchaser should have been aware of the equitable interest had reasonable enquiries been made
- Imputed notice means that if the agent or employee of the purchaser had notice then the purchaser will also have notice.

REVISION NOTE

If you are studying land law or have studied it then go back to your land law materials and check what it says on notice. See *Land Law* in the Law Express Series, especially Chapters 1 and 2.

Judicature Acts 1873 and 1875 and the question of fusion

The Judicature Acts abolished both the old common law courts and the Court of Chancery and replaced them with a new Supreme Court consisting of the High Court and the Court of Appeal. The Judicature Act 1873 provided that where equity and the common law conflict then equity shall prevail (s. 25(11)). The passage of this Act led to a debate which is still not settled on the extent to which equity and the common law are fused.

The question of whether equity and the common law are fused or not is a very familiar area for exam questions. It is an issue which is still debated and so there is no right answer – do not feel that you have to come to one!

Fusion can mean two things:

1 That the *administration* of equity and the common law is fused. This is so as all divisions of the High Court have jurisdiction in both common law and equity unlike before when only the Court of Chancery exercised equitable jurisdiction.
2 That the actual systems of common law and equity have been fused so that it is no longer correct to speak of common law and equity but of one system. This aspect has given rise to debate. Lord Diplock in *United Scientific Holdings* v *Burnley BC* [1978] considered that law and equity are fused, in contrast to the well-known

statement of Ashburner in *Principles of Equity* (1933) who compared law and equity to separate streams which although running side by side 'do not mingle their waters'. In fact, there has been a vigorous growth in equity since the middle years of the twentieth century. See, for example, the fiduciary concept (Chapter 9), the law on trusts of the home (Chapter 9) and equitable doctrines and remedies (Chapter 2).

EXAM TIP

When reading this book, make a note of the areas where equity's intervention has been more marked as indicated above as this could form the basis of an answer on equity. Try to include examples from as wide a range as possible. This is dealt with in more detail below.

The question of fusion is somewhat out of date now and exam questions may instead ask you if law and equity ought to exist as separate systems of law at all.

 Make your answer stand out

The debate on the future of equity as a separate system and if it is necessary to regard equitable and common law jurisdiction as distinct is current at the moment and you must be aware of it for the exam. Sarah Worthington in her book *Equity* (2006) argues strongly for the end of two distinct systems. She points out that the origin of equity is to be found in history and not policy. This is unarguable but it is easy to forget that it is so. For a view that trusts do not need to exist under a system of equitable duties and rights see Honore (2003).

What is clear is that the Judicature Acts did fuse the administration of law and equity.

KEY CASE

Walsh v *Lonsdale* (1882) 21 Ch D 9 (HC)

Concerning: effect of the Judicature Acts

Facts

A lease was granted but not by deed. Thus it was only equitable – an agreement for a lease can be enforced by equity on the basis of the maxim that 'equity looks on that as done which ought to be done', i.e. if a person has agreed to grant a lease then they ought to do so and, as far as possible, equity will assume that they have done so.

Legal principle

The Court applied s.25(11) of the Judicature Act 1873 and held that, as equity prevailed, there was an equitable lease.

■ Modern equity – developments since 1875

This is a likely area for exam questions and you will find the following chapters particularly useful:

- Chapter 2: Equitable remedies and doctrines
- Chapters 8 and 9: Resulting trusts and Constructive trusts – especially thinking about how the constructive trust can be used
- Chapter 9: The section on Trusts of the home – the extent to which equity has recognised rights here has been one of the best modern examples of equity.

Note also the following:

- The extent to which equity is flourishing in Australia (e.g. see *Queensland Mines Ltd* v *Hudson* (1978) in Chapter 9
- In various cases judges are starting to base their decisions on wider grounds (e.g. unconscionability) see, for example, *Pennington* v *Waine* (2002) in Chapter 6
- How judges often today seem more forward looking than, for example, judges in the 1950s (e.g. see the judgments of Lord Simonds in a number of charity cases in Chapter 10 such as *Oppenheim* v *Tobacco Securities Trust Co. Ltd* and *Gilmour* v *Coates).*
- The variety of uses to which trusts are put – this is dealt with more fully in one of the model answers on the companion website.

■ Chapter summary: putting it all together

Test yourself

- ☐ Can you tick all the points from the **revision checklist** at the beginning of this chapter?
- ☐ Attempt the **sample question** from the beginning of this chapter using the answer guidelines below.
- ☐ Go to the **companion website** to access more revision support online, including interactive quizzes, sample questions with answer guidelines, 'you be the marker' exercises, flashcards and podcasts you can download.

Answer guidelines

See the essay question at the start of this chapter.

Approaching the question

You need to select no more than four areas and look at the contribution of equity. Never make the mistake of trying to say something about everything: you will end up by not saying anything worth saying about anything!

Important points to include

This is up to you so long as you make sure that:

- You relate the points you make to the question
- You link them to each other so that the essay has a theme.

Some ideas on what to include are:

- Trusts of the family home. How did equity intervene? What did it do that the common law could not have done?
- Secret trusts – obviously the common law would not have enforced these – explain why. Do not just explain what a secret trust is but say why you feel that it is/is not right that equity should enforce them.
- Constructive trusts – same approach as with secret trusts – take a case such as *Boardman* v *Phipps* – consider the response of the common law and then that of equity. Here you have an interesting point as it could be argued that in this case equity set the standard of the trustee's fiduciary duty too high. Learn some key phrases from both the majority and dissenting judgments in the House of Lords and integrate them into your answer.

 Make your answer stand out

End by referring to the debate about the place of equity – although it may have made a great contribution in the past is there a need for it today? Does the common law recognise issues of conscience? Is it capable of doing so?

READ TO IMPRESS

Ashburner, W. (1933) *Principles of Equity*, 2nd edn, London: Butterworths.

Duddington, J. (2006) *Essentials of Equity and Trusts*, Harlow: Pearson Education.

Hanbury and Martin, J. (2009) *Modern Equity*, 18th edn, London: Sweet and Maxwell.

Hayton, D. and Marshall, O. (2005) *The Law of Trusts and Equitable Remedies*, 17th edn, London: Sweet and Maxwell.

Honore, T. (2003) 'Trusts, the Inessentials' in *Rationalizing Property, Equity and Trusts: Essays in Honour of Edward Burn*, ed. Getzler, J., London: Lexis Nexis.

Hopkins, N. (2006) 'Conscience, discretion and the creation of property rights', 26 LS 475.

Mason, A. (1994) 'The Place of Equity and Equitable Remedies in the Common Law World', 110 LQR 238.

Watt (2009) *'Equity Stirring; the Story of Justice Beyond Law'*, Oxford: Hart Publishing.

Worthington, S. (2006) *Equity*, 2nd edn, Oxford: Oxford University Press.

NOTES

NOTES

Equitable remedies and doctrines

2

Revision checklist

Essential points you should know:

- [ ] the characteristics of equitable remedies
- [ ] the situations in which a grant of the remedies of injunction, specific performance, rescission and rectification would be appropriate
- [ ] the meaning of undue influence
- [ ] the situations when undue influence is presumed and when it is not
- [ ] the effect of undue influence (and misrepresentation) on third parties

■ Topic map

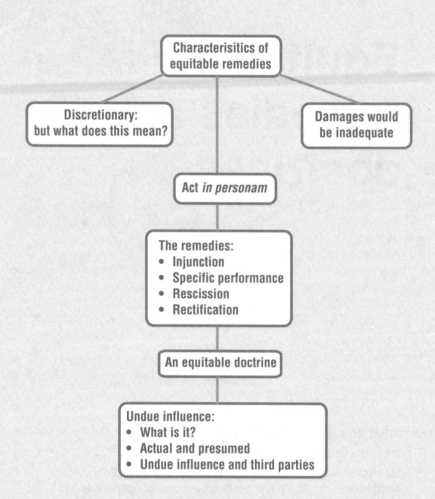

∎Introduction

This is not a difficult topic but you should check if your syllabus includes it.

If it is just 'trusts' it will not. However, syllabuses for those courses where the final qualification gives exemption from the academic stage of qualifying as a barrister or solicitor (i.e. a qualifying law degree) must include equity other than trusts and so it is almost certain that you will be examined on equity as such.

Essay questions An essay will often deal with equitable remedies and may ask you to consider them in the light of a particular quotation. This should not pose great problems of understanding; rather the problem is often the amount of material to hand and the consequent danger of simply ploughing through it with no real attempt to answer the question. The golden rule applies: make a selection of material and then use it to address the issues raised in the question. Nothing more! Other possibilities are essays on undue influence, especially the decision in *Barclays Bank* v *O'Brien* (1994), and on the developing case law on breach of confidence.

Problem questions Problem questions are less likely on the remedies although possible ones could be on specific performance, freezing and/or search orders.

A more likely area is undue influence where there are various issues to explore and this is the area chosen for a problem question on the companion website to this chapter.

■ Sample question

Could you answer this question? Below is a typical essay question that could arise on this topic. Guidelines on answering the question are included at the end of this chapter, while a sample problem question and guidance on tackling it can be found on the companion website.

ESSAY QUESTION

'Equitable remedies are discretionary.'

Do you agree?

■ Characteristics of equitable remedies

1 *They are discretionary*, whereas the common law remedy of damages is available as of right. This does not, however, mean that everything is left to the discretion of the court in each case: as we shall see, there are clear principles governing the grant of equitable remedies.
2 *They are granted where the common law remedies (e.g. damages) would be inadequate* or where the common law remedies are not available because the right is exclusively equitable (e.g. a right of a beneficiary under a trust).
3 *They act in personam*, i.e. against the defendant personally.

Points (1) and (2) are illustrated by the case of *Patel* v *Ali* [1984].

REVISION NOTE

Go back to Chapter 1 and check that you are familiar with this case. It is an excellent illustration of equitable remedies.

In *Patel* v *Ali* (1984) you can see that:

■ Equitable remedies, although discretionary, are not granted at the whim of the court: note the phrase 'hardship amounting to injustice' as the principle here.
■ Damages could be granted to compensate the buyer.

The next section will look at the main remedies.

■ Injunctions

This is a court order requiring a party either to do or not to do a particular act.

An **injunction** may be used:

■ to restrain a breach of contract

■ to restrain the commission of a tort (e.g. a nuisance or a trespass)

■ to restrain a breach of confidence

■ to restrain a breach of trust

■ in matrimonial and family matters. (The Family Law Act 1996 gives the courts extensive powers to grant injunctions in divorce proceedings.)

Perpetual injunctions

Perpetual injunctions will not necessarily last forever but they are final in that they will finally resolve the issue between the parties. There are two types of perpetual injunction:

1 *Prohibitory*, i.e. restraining the doing of an act.
2 *Mandatory*, i.e. commanding the doing of an act.

Interlocutory injunctions

The object of an interlocutory injunction is to preserve the status quo until the trial of an action, for example, to restrain an association from holding a meeting without allowing certain members to attend (*Woodford* v *Smith* (1970)).

They may be:

■ prohibitory (see above)

■ mandatory (see above), or

■ *quia timet.*

A *quia timet* injunction is granted to restrain a threatened apprehended injury to the claimant's rights even though no injury has yet occurred. For example, in *Torquay Hotel Co. Ltd.* v *Cousins* (1969) the defendants, members of a trade union, intended to picket the claimant's hotel to prevent the delivery of fuel oil that would interfere with the execution of contracts which the claimants had made for the supply of fuel oil. A *quia timet* injunction was granted.

Interlocutory injunctions are often granted without notice to the other side – the old term for this was *ex parte*.

Principles on the grant of interlocutory injunctions

KEY CASE

American Cyanamid Co. v Ethicon Ltd. **[1975] AC 396 (HL)**

Concerning: principles on which an interlocutory injunction will be granted

Facts

There was an application for a *quia timet* injunction to prevent the infringement of a patent.

Legal principles

The court laid down the following principles to be followed when deciding to grant an interlocutory injunction:

(a) Is there a serious question to be tried? If the defendant has no arguable defence at all then an injunction will be granted and points (b) and (c) below do not arise. Otherwise the court will consider the following points:

(b) If there is a serious issue, will damages be an adequate remedy so that an injunction will not be needed? This must be looked at from the point of view of:

   (i) The claimant, i.e. would damages be adequate compensation for loss caused to him by acts of the defendant before the trial?

   (ii) The defendant, i.e. if the claimant loses at the trial then could any loss to the defendant be compensated by the claimant giving an undertaking in damages?

(c) If damages would be inadequate, then should an injunction be granted taking into account the balance of convenience to each party? *Hubbard* v *Pitt* (1976) illustrates both (b) and (c).

(d) There may be other special factors to be considered as in the American Cyanamid case itself, where an interlocutory injunction was granted to prevent infringement of a patent for a pharmaceutical product. The argument was that if the defendant's product had been used prior to the trial, and the claimant then obtained a permanent injunction against its further marketing, the claimant would themselves lose goodwill. Accordingly the interlocutory injunction prevented the defendants from marketing the product at all.

Freezing order

This is an interlocutory injunction designed to prevent the defendant from disposing of assets which would otherwise be available to meet the claimant's claim or removing them from the courts' jurisdiction. The order is often known as a *Mareva* order from the decision in *Mareva Compania Naviera SA* v *International Bulkcarriers SA* [1980].

The general principles laid down in the *American Cyanimid* case apply to when this remedy will be granted. Also, the claimant should:

■ Have a good arguable case.

■ Make full and frank disclosure of all material matters together with full particulars of his claim and its amount and should state fairly the points made against it by the defendant.

■ Normally give grounds for believing that the defendants have assets in the jurisdiction. All assets are within the scope of a freezing order which has thus been ordered in relation to, for example, bank accounts (the most frequent situation), motor vehicles, jewellery and goodwill.

■ Normally give grounds for believing either that the assets will be removed from the jurisdiction before the claim is satisfied or that in some way they might be dissipated.

Search order

These allow search of premises of a possible defendant and are especially useful where a defendant might destroy evidence once a claim form was served on him. They are used, for example, in cases of alleged video pirating.

In *Anton Piller KG* v *Manufacturing Processes Ltd* (1976), Omrod LJ laid down the following conditions which must be satisfied by the claimant for the grant of the order:

■ an extremely strong prima facie case

■ actual or potential damage of a very serious nature

■ clear evidence that the defendant has incriminating documents or things and a real possibility of their destruction before an application without notice can be made.

Make your answer stand out

Search orders were criticised on the ground that they could allow oppressive conduct, amounting to the ransacking of a business, when there was no case proved against that person. See Dockray and Laddie (1990) and, for a case example, *Lock International plc* v *Beswick* (1989).

In *Universal Thermosensors* v *Hibben* (1992) conditions were imposed on the use of these search orders which have now been incorporated into the standard form (see also Practice Direction Civil Practice Rules 25 para 7).

EXAM TIP

Freezing, and especially search orders, are an area where there is room for debate about the need to consider the interests of the party seeking the order and the party against whom it is being sought. Think about this issue for an essay question.

■ Specific performance

KEY DEFINITION: Specific performance

This is an order requiring the performance of obligations under a contract. Whereas injunctions are generally negative (you must not), SP is positive (you must).

EXAM TIP

Exam questions are likely to focus on the circumstances when an order of **specific performance (SP)** may be granted so look in detail at pairs of slightly contrasting cases and read round them to see if you can discover any principle. Do not learn masses of cases superficially but those you learn, learn well!

! Don't be tempted to...

Be careful you don't overlook the distinction between injunctions and specific performance. Some cases appear to deal with injunctions and not SP even though they appear in textbooks under the heading of SP. This is because there is an overlap:

- SP: you must carry out the contract
- Injunction: you must not fail to carry out the contract

Therefore, in an exam question on SP you will gain extra marks for bringing in cases involving injunctions which illustrate this overlap.

The fundamental principle is that SP will not normally be granted in certain situations.

EXAM TIP

Note the use of the word 'normally' in the above sentence. Remember that equity is a discretionary system and so there are fewer black and white rules than in other areas of the law.

These are:
- Where damages would be an adequate remedy

KEY CASE

Sky Petroleum v *VIP Petroleum* **[1974] 1 WLR 576**

Concerning: grant of an injunction, which would amount to specific performance, where damages would not be an adequate remedy

Facts

During a petrol shortage the defendants terminated their contract with the claimants to supply them with petrol.

Legal principle

An injunction was granted restraining the defendants from withholding supplies of petrol. There was a petrol shortage at the time and so, if only damages had been awarded to the claimants, they would have been unlikely to obtain supplies elsewhere.

- Where constant supervision would be needed by the court

KEY CASE

Co-operative Insurance Society v Argyll Stores (Holdings) Ltd [1998] AC 1 (HL)
Concerning: principles to be applied when granting specific performance

Facts

Specific performance was sought of an undertaking to keep a supermarket open during the usual hours of business in a lease which had still 19 years to run. The supermarket was an 'anchor store' in a shopping centre and its closure would badly affect the viability of the rest of the centre.

Legal principle

The House of Lords considered that if the store was ordered to be kept open the loss to the tenant would exceed that which would be suffered by the landlord if the supermarket closed. In addition, the principle that the court would need to supervise any order of SP remained important.

 Make your answer stand out

This decision was regarded as a setback by those who favour an extension of this remedy (e.g. see Phang (1998).

■ Where the contract is for personal services.

KEY STATUTE

Trade Union and Labour Relations Act 1992, s. 236

This prohibits the courts from enforcing performance of contracts of employment either by specific performance or injunction. This only applies to actual contracts of employment, not to other contracts of personal service. See *Page One Records* v *Britton (t/a The Troggs)* [1967] and *Warren* v *Mendy* (1989).

Warner Bros Pictures Inc. v *Nelson* [1937] 1 KB 209 (HC)

Concerning: use of an injunction in contracts of personal service

Facts

The actress (Bette Davis) agreed not to work as an actress for another film company for the period of her contract with Warner Bros.

Legal principle

The injunction would be granted on the ground that Miss Davis could earn a living doing other work. It would not force her to work for Warner Bros.

You should also consider that there have been instances where the courts have enforced a contract for personal services against an employer, i.e. where it has ordered the contract of employment to continue. However, these have been in unusual circumstances as in *Hill* v *CA Parsons* (1972).

■ Rescission

KEY DEFINITION: Rescission

This remedy restores the parties to their position before the contract or other transaction was made.

EXAM TIP

You are unlikely to get a detailed question on this but a knowledge of it is useful as it is the normal remedy in cases of undue influence.

■ Rectification

KEY DEFINITION: Rectification

Where a written instrument (e.g. a contract) does not accord with the actual intentions of the parties it can be made to do so by an order of rectification.

Craddock Bros. v *Hunt* [1923] 2 Ch 136 (HC)

Concerning: rectification

Facts

A conveyance of a house included the adjacent yard, which actually belonged to another house.

Legal principle

The conveyance would be rectified to exclude the yard.

Equitable doctrines

We will now consider the doctrine of undue influence.

There are other equitable doctrines but you are less likely to be asked questions on them. Their names, so that you can check if they are on your syllabus, are:

- conversion
- reconversion
- election
- performance
- satisfaction

Undue influence

Undue influence is a doctrine that, by its nature, is difficult to define precisely but in essence it aims to prevent the vulnerable from exploitation. It is really directed at the manner in which a transaction is entered into.

Example 2.1

A wealthy elderly lady, Florence, has become a recluse and relies for advice on her accountant, Tom, who is the only person she sees regularly apart from her carers. She tells the accountant that she intends to make a will but has no one to leave her property to. Tom says that he will give the matter some thought and, in the course of many conversations, gradually persuades her to leave a substantial part of her property to him. A straightforward example of undue influence is *Re Craig* (1971).

KEY CASE

Royal Bank of Scotland v *Etridge* (No. 2) [2001] UKHL 44 (HL)
Concerning: what is undue influence?

Facts
The facts of this case do not aid an understanding of the legal principle.

Legal principle
Lord Nicholls (HL) held that there is a distinction between:

(a) cases of actual coercion
(b) cases where the undue influence arises from a particular relationship.

In (b) there is a subdivision between:

(i) Cases where there is a relationship of trust and confidence between two people. If it is established that there has been a transaction which calls for some explanation then the burden shifts to the person seeking to uphold the transaction to produce evidence to counter the inference of undue influence.
(ii) Certain types of relationship where one party has acquired influence over another who is vulnerable and dependent and by whom substantial gifts are not normally to be expected (e.g. parent and child, trustee and beneficiary and medical adviser and patient). In these cases there is a presumption of undue influence by the stronger party over the weaker. *Goodchild* v *Bradbury* (2006) appears to be an example of this category.

Note *Shaw* v *Finnemore* (2009): a recent example of a finding of undue influence.

EXAM TIP

The most likely area of undue influence for problem questions is (b)(ii) above. It should be noted that (b)(i) does not include husband and wife, a common scenario for exam problems and so this situation would fall into (b)(ii).

! Don't be tempted to...

Make sure that, having first decided that this is a possible undue influence case, you then move on immediately to see where in the above categories it falls. This will decide the rest of the case as it is vital to know if undue influence has to be proved or not.

Undue influence and third parties

This area has become of great importance in recent years especially since the decision of the House of Lords in *Barclays Bank* v *O'Brien* (1994).

Students often jump straight to this issue when they see it in a problem question and do not first ask if there has been undue influence in the first place. Do this first!

Example 2.2

John persuades Claud his partner, to enter into a second mortgage of their jointly owned home to the Viper Bank in order to secure some business debts of John. It is clear that John exercised undue influence over Claud to persuade him to sign. The question is whether the Viper Bank is affected by what John has done. If it is not, then although John may be liable to Claud the actual mortgage is unaffected.

EXAM TIP

The principles stated by Lord Browne-Wilkinson in *Barclays Bank* v *O'Brien* (1994) were the starting point of the law here. However, they have been overtaken by those stated by Lord Nicholls in *Etridge* (below) and in a problem question you should concentrate on applying these.

Note: In the case below the word 'surety' is used and here it means the person who has agreed to guarantee the debt, etc.: Claud in the above example.

KEY CASE

Royal Bank of Scotland v *Etridge* (No. 2) [2002] 2 AC 773 (HL)

Concerning: (a) when a lender is put on inquiry and (b) steps which a lender should take to avoid being affected by the undue influence of another (e.g. the borrower)

Facts

The facts of this case do not aid an understanding of the legal principle.

Legal principles

These were stated by Lord Nicholls as follows:

(a) A lender is put on inquiry when one person offers to stand surety for the debts of:
  ■ his or her spouse

■ a person involved in a non-commercial relationship with the surety and the lender is aware of this

■ any company in which any of the above hold shares.

(b) Steps to be taken when a lender is put on inquiry:
  ■ The lender must contact the surety and request that they nominate a solicitor
  ■ The surety must reply nominating a solicitor
  ■ The lender must, with the consent of the surety, disclose to the solicitor all relevant information – both the debtor's financial position and the details of the proposed loan
  ■ The solicitor must advise the surety in a face-to-face meeting at which the debtor is not present. The advice must cover an explanation of the documentation, the risks to the surety in signing and emphasise that the surety must decide whether to proceed
  ■ The solicitor must, if satisfied that the surety wishes to proceed, send written confirmation to the lender that the solicitor has explained the nature of the documents and their implications for the surety.

✓ Make your answer stand out

The principle in *O'Brien* and the decision in *Etridge* (above) have been the subject of a great deal of academic debate. A good place to start is the article by Andrews (2002).

Consequences of undue influence

If the transaction is affected by undue influence then it is voidable.

❗ Don't be tempted to...

Be sure you consider the *extent* to which the mortgage is set aside:

■ *TSB* v *Camfield* (1995): the whole mortgage was set aside

■ *Dunbar Bank plc* v *Nadeem* (1997): it was only set aside on condition that the claimant accounted to the mortgagee for the benefit which she had from it.

Misrepresentation and undue influence

Instead of, or in addition to, the possibility of undue influence an exam question may ask you if there has been misrepresentation. You will probably not need to remember so much on this as you did in your contract days, but do note the definition:

KEY DEFINITION: Misrepresentation

This is an untrue statement of fact which induces a person to enter into a transaction.

Look out for where undue influence and **misrepresentation** are possibly combined: i.e. X uses undue influence to persuade Y, his partner, to sign a mortgage but also lies about how much, for example, the mortgage is for.

 Make your answer stand out

Read 'Mortgages and Undue Influence' (Thompson, 2003). It provides an excellent critical study of the law.

■Chapter summary: putting it all together

Test yourself

- ☐ Can you tick all the points from the **revision checklist** at the beginning of this chapter?
- ☐ Attempt the **sample question** from the beginning of this chapter using the answer guidelines below.
- ☐ Go to the **companion website** to access more revision support online, including interactive quizzes, sample questions with answer guidelines, 'you be the marker' exercises, flashcards and podcasts you can download.

Answer guidelines

See the essay question at the start of this chapter.

Approaching the question

This is a very typical one in equity exams and requires you to think about the nature of equitable remedies. What you must *not* do is to just plough through the remedies summarising them!

Important points to include

Start with an introduction which addresses the issue: what is meant by discretionary? Look back to *Patel* v *Ali* and discuss how the word 'discretionary' was applied. The essential point is that, although there are no rigid rules about when equitable remedies will be granted and refused, there are principles.

Now go on to select cases illustrating principles in the grant of equitable remedies – look back through the material in this chapter and select cases which you think that you can use and then research them.

 Make your answer stand out

Go to Chapter 9 on constructive trusts and refer to the remedial constructive trust. This is said to be a remedy. Is it? If it is, it is certainly discretionary but what are the principles which govern its exercise? Are there any?

READ TO IMPRESS

Andrews, G. (2002) 'Undue Influence – Where's the disadvantage?', 66 Conv. 456.

Dockray, M. and Laddie, H. (1990) 'Piller Problems', 106 LQR 661.

Phang, A. (1998) 'Specific Performance – Explaining the Roots of Settled Practice', 61 MLR 421.

Thompson, M. (2003) 'Mortgages and Undue Influence', in *Modern Studies in Property Law*, (ed. Cooke), 2nd edn, Oxford: Hart Publishing.

NOTES

The three certainties

3

Revision checklist

Essential points you should know:

- [ ] why the certainties are needed
- [ ] what the three certainties are
- [ ] the distinction between fixed and discretionary trusts
- [ ] the distinction between where property is left on trust and where there is a conditional gift
- [ ] the effect of a clause which attempts to cure uncertainty

■ Topic map

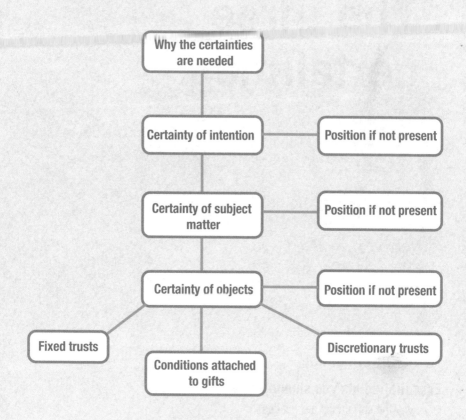

■Introduction

This is not a difficult area and often appears in exam questions.

Three certainties questions usually involve clauses in **wills** although certainties issues can arise in *inter vivos* gifts also.

There are two reasons for requiring certainty in the creation of a trust:

1 A practical one. It would be wrong for the court to impose a trust where none was intended. Trusteeship can be an onerous task and so no one should be held a trustee unless this was clearly intended.
2 The need for the court to be able to control the trust (*Morice* v *Bishop of Durham* (1805)).

ASSESSMENT ADVICE

Essay questions Essay questions are likely to deal with any of these areas, all of which have led to a great deal of academic debate:

■ Certainty of subject matter where the goods are not yet ascertained as in *Re London Wine Co.* (1986) (see later in this chapter)

■ The tests for certainty of objects, especially in discretionary trusts but also possibly in fixed trusts and where there is a condition precedent

■ The decisions in *McPhail* v *Doulton* [1971] and *Re Barlow's Will Trusts* (1979) are worth looking at in detail. Make sure that you understand the debates surrounding them.

Problem questions The three certainties is one of the favourite areas for problem questions. These are not difficult to gain a reasonable pass on but if you are looking for a really good mark you need to go deeper than just running through the requirements of certainty and concentrate on discussing any problematic areas such as those mentioned in the essay question advice above. You can also boost your mark in answering problem questions by paying very close attention to the actual words used in the creation of a trust and analysing them very carefully. To sum up: this is a good area to aim to score highly on.

■ Sample question

Could you answer this question? Below is a typical problem question that could arise on this topic. An outline answer is included at the end of the chapter, while a sample essay question and guidance on tackling it can be found on the companion website.

PROBLEM QUESTION

Susan, who died recently, left a will containing the following bequests:

1 £250,000 to my husband, John, safe in the knowledge that he will provide for our children.
2 £10,000 to my daughter, Barbara, provided that she allows my sister, Eileen, a reasonable sum each year to provide her with a few of the little comforts of life.
3 My collection of rare books shall be available for any friend of mine who wishes to select a book in memory of me.
4 £300,000 to be distributed, at the discretion of my trustees, among employees, ex-employees, their friends and relations of my late husband's company, Midland Optical Illusion Ltd.

Can you advise Arthur, Susan's **executor**, on the validity of these gifts?

■ What are the three certainties?

These are:

- certainty of intention to create a trust
- certainty of the subject matter of the trust
- certainty of the objects of the trust.

These requirements have been set out in many cases, for example, by Lord Langdale in *Knight* v *Knight* (1840).

Certainty of intention

Certainty of intention means that the person who is given the property shall hold it on trust, i.e. it is evidence that the settlor or testator intended to impose a binding obligation that the property was to be held on trust. Often common sense and an ability to see clearly what precise words and phrases mean is enough when answering a problem question.

Example 3.1

(a) John by will leaves £1000 to Albert and says that he would like Albert to look after his children.
(b) John leaves £1000 to Albert on trust for his children.

It is obvious that (b) is a trust but that (a) is not. Why? Because in (a) there is only a request. It is often said that 'precatory words do not create a trust'. Precatory words are words such as request, hope and desire which do not impose a trust and where the recipient can keep the property as a gift. A good example is *Re Diggles* (1888) where the word desire did not create a trust.

EXAM TIP

■ Use your common sense – do the words used look like the imposition of a trust?
■ Look at all the words used – not just particular ones.

Compare the following cases:

KEY CASE

Re Adams and Kensington Vestry **(1884) 27 Ch D 394 (CA)**
Concerning: certainty of intention

Facts
The testator gave his estate to his wife 'in full confidence that she will do what is right as the disposal thereof between my children …'.

Legal principle
The words 'in full confidence' did not create a trust.

KEY CASE

Comiskey v *Bowring-Hanbury* **[1905] AC 84 (HL)**
Concerning: certainty of intention

Facts
A testator gave his property to his wife 'in full confidence that at her death she will devise it to one or more of my nieces as she shall think fit'. If she did not do ▶

this then the will directed that the property should be divided equally among the nieces. It was held that this created a trust.

Legal principle

Look at the meaning of the words used taken as a whole and not in isolation. Although the words 'in full confidence' were used here as in *Adams* (above), here the second sentence was clearly mandatory and so created a trust.

Re Harding (2007) EWHC 3 (HC)

Concerning: certainty of intention to create a trust

Facts

The testatrix's will said that it was her wish that all she possessed should be taken by the Roman Catholic Diocese of Westminster to hold in trust for the Black Community in four London Boroughs. Did these words create a trust?

Legal principle

The court held that they did. Although the word 'wish' was in itself precatory the will did use the word 'trust' later.

Note also *Wallbank and Wallbank* v *Price* (2008): It was argued that the word 'should' in a document which was executed was merely precatory and did not create a trust. However, the court held that it was sufficient and applied the wider approach as evidenced by *Paul* v *Constance* – below.

 Make your answer stand out

Learn some more modern examples of equity in this area (e.g. *R* v *Clowes* (No. 2) [1994]). This also illustrates a link between equity and the law of theft: you can impress the examiner with your knowledge of this! In *Duggan* v *Governor of Full Sutton Prison* (2004) it was held that when prisoners' money was put in a fund under the control of the governor there was no intention to create a trust of that money for the prisoners. *Paul* v *Constance* [1977] (see Chapter 6) is a good example for exams as you can combine it with a discussion of constitution of trusts. See *Re Farepak Food and Gifts Ltd* (*in administration*) (2006) in Chapter 8. This is an excellent case for essay questions as it contains material on express, resulting and constructive trusts.

The *effect* of the lack of certainty of intention is that the donee (no trustee here) takes the property as an absolute gift.

Certainty of subject matter

This is a simple enough point: there is no point in creating a trust by showing certainty of intention if we do not know what property is to be held on trust.

KEY CASE

Anthony v *Donges* (1998) 2 FLR 775 (HC)
Concerning: certainty of subject matter

Facts
A widow was left 'such minimal part of the estate as she might be entitled to ... for maintenance purposes'.

Legal principle
There was no certainty of subject matter.

See also *Palmer* v *Simmonds* (1854): 'the bulk of my estate' was too uncertain.

KEY CASE

Re Golay [1965] 1 WLR 969
Concerning: apparent lack of certainty of subject matter

Facts
Executors under a will were directed to allow a beneficiary 'to enjoy the use of one of my flats and receive a reasonable income from my other properties'.

Legal principle
Although the word 'reasonable' seemed too uncertain the gift was upheld as the court assumed that it referred to the beneficiaries' previous standard of living.

KEY CASE

Curtis v *Rippon* (1820) 5 Madd 434 (HC)

Concerning: the possibility that a person is intended to be a trustee of part but to receive the other part as a gift

Facts

A widow received all her husband's property subject to a trust where she was to 'use the property for her spiritual and temporal good and that of the children, remembering always according to circumstances the Church of God and the poor'. It was held that as the shares to be taken by the children, the Church and the poor were uncertain, the widow took all as there was no doubt that she was intended to benefit to some extent.

Legal principle

Where the shares to be taken by the beneficiaries are uncertain but there is also an absolute gift (often to the intended trustee) then the gift takes effect.

Students sometimes say at this point: 'But it is a fundamental principle that a trustee cannot benefit from the trust.' Quite right. But the point is that there is no trust as there is no certainty of subject matter.

KEY CASE

Re London Wine Co. Shippers Ltd [1986] PCC 121 (HC)

Concerning: certainty of subject matter where goods are unascertained

Facts

Buyers of wine which was stored at a warehouse claimed that it was held on trust for them but the claim failed as the wine had not been separated from a larger stock of similar wine held at the warehouse.

Legal principle

Trust property must be ascertainable.

 Make your answer stand out

Look also, for example, at *Hunter* v *Moss* (1994) and *Re Goldcorp Exchange Ltd (in receivership)* [1995]. Read the criticism of *Hunter* v *Moss* by Hayton (1994).

The *effect* of the lack of certainty of subject matter is:

- if there is no certainty of what the subject matter is then there can be no trust as there is nothing to hold on trust
- if the attempted trust has been attached to a gift then the gift becomes absolute as in *Curtis* v *Rippon* (1820) (above).

Certainty of objects (i.e. beneficiaries)

Note at the outset that the rules differ depending on the type of trust (see Figure 3.1):

Figure 3.1

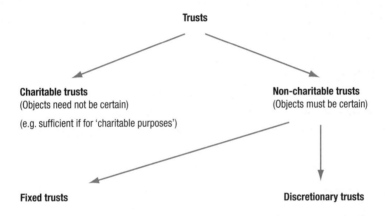

This chapter will deal with non-charitable trusts (private trusts) as one exam question would be unlikely to deal with certainties in both charitable and non-charitable trusts.

REVISION NOTE

Check Chapter 10 for certainty of objects in charitable trusts.

It is vital that you recognise and can apply the distinction between fixed and discretionary trusts.

■ Fixed trusts

KEY DEFINITION: Fixed trust

Where the interests in the trust property are fixed in the trust instrument.

Example 3.2

'To all my children in equal shares.'

Here there is no room for any discretion by the trustees.

KEY DEFINITION: Rule for certainty of objects in fixed trusts

All the beneficiaries must be capable of being listed, i.e. there must be no doubt as to who the beneficiaries are: *IRC* v *Broadway Cottages Trust* (1955).

This is really common sense when applied to the above example. Each child is to have an equal amount and so the division cannot be made until we know how many to divide the sum by.

Discretionary trusts

KEY DEFINITION: Discretionary trust

Where the trustees have a discretion as to whether a person will be a beneficiary or not.

KEY CASE

McPhail v *Doulton* [1971] AC 424 (HL)

Concerning: certainty of objects in discretionary trusts

Facts

A trust provided that the trustees were to apply the income from a fund at their absolute discretion for the benefit of any officers and employees of a (named) company together with ex-officers and ex-employees and their relatives and dependants. This was sufficiently certain.

Legal principle

In discretionary trusts the test for certainty of objects is: 'Can it be said with certainty that any given individual is or is not a member of the class?' (Lord Wilberforce)

KEY DEFINITION: Rule for certainty of objects in discretionary trusts

'Can it be said with certainty that any given individual is or is not a member of the class?'

As you can see from the facts it would be impossible to list all the beneficiaries (e.g. who are the relatives?). However, it must be possible to say with certainty if a particular person is a beneficiary.

Example 3.3

A gift to my old mates. This does not satisfy the test of certainty as it is not possible to say with certainty if anyone is an old mate.

Example 3.4

A gift to my cousins. This does satisfy the test, as it is possible to say with certainty if a person is a cousin.

Conceptual and evidential uncertainty

Re Baden's Deed Trusts (No. 2) [1973] distinguished between conceptual and evidential uncertainty. Example 3.3 is a case of conceptual uncertainty in that the whole concept of a mate is not capable of precise definition and so the gift will fail. Example 3.4 is an example of evidential uncertainty in that it may be difficult to establish who is a cousin but that is no bar to a person coming forward and proving that she *is* a cousin.

Effect of a lack of certainty

Provided that the other two certainties are present the property will be held on a resulting trust for the settlor or, if the trust is created by will, then for the testator's estate.

Note these other points in certainty of objects in discretionary trusts:

- *Trustees have a duty to appreciate the 'width of the field'* (Megarry VC in *Re Hay's Settlement Trusts* [1982]). This means that although they cannot draw up a complete list of the objects they should not distribute the property until they have decided if the selection is to be made 'merely from a dozen or instead, thousands or millions'.

- There is some authority for saying that the trust will not be enforced if the width of objects makes it 'administratively unworkable'. In *R v District Auditor, ex parte West Yorkshire MCC* [1986] a trust for the inhabitants of West Yorkshire (about 2.5 million people) failed on this ground.

■ Power to cure uncertainty

This can arise in two situations:

(a) Where there is uncertainty about a particular *fact*. A third party can be made judge of this.

KEY CASE

Re Tuck's Settlement Trusts [1978] Ch 49 (HC)

Concerning: decision on whether a person satisfies a criteria to be made by a third party

Facts

A chief rabbi was made judge of whether a person was of Jewish blood.

Legal principle

This was valid as the decision was to be based on measurable criteria.

(b) Where there is conceptual uncertainty.

Example 3.5

John's will provides that each of his old drinking pals at the Black Bush shall have a bottle of whisky and that, in case of doubt, the landlord of the Black Bush shall have the power to decide who they are.

Given that the phrase 'old drinking pals at the Black Bush' is conceptually uncertain, does the power given to the landlord save it?

The probability is that this would not save the gift as the point is that the phrase itself is conceptually uncertain and so a power to decide is irrelevant: What can the landlord decide? In addition, the court cannot control the trust (e.g. see *Re Jones* [1953]).

■ Conditions precedent and certainty of objects

Re Barlow's Will Trusts (1979) 1 WLR 278 (HC)

Concerning: certainty of objects where there is a condition precedent

Facts

A will directed that a friend of the testator should be allowed to purchase any of her paintings. The court held that a friend was a person who had met the testator frequently when circumstances allowed on a social and not a business occasion. On this basis the gift was allowed to stand.

Legal principle

Gifts subject to conditions precedent are subject to a less strict test than those in discretionary trusts as the amount which one person receives does not affect what others will receive.

 Make your answer stand out

This case is controversial and you should be prepared to discuss whether it is correct. See Emery (1982) for an excellent article that goes to the heart of the issues.

Students often apply the test in *Re Barlow's Will Trusts* [1979] whenever they see the word 'friend' in a question. This may be wrong. If £100 is left to be shared on discretionary trust 'among all my friends' this would fail as the test in *McPhail* v *Doulton* (1971) would apply and 'friends' would not satisfy it.

■ The rule against perpetuities and discretionary trusts

REVISION NOTE

This rule is dealt with in Chapter 4 but for now just remember that it may come up in a certainties question!

■ Chapter summary: putting it all together

Test yourself

☐ Can you tick all the points from the **revision checklist** at the beginning of this chapter?

☐ Attempt the **sample question** from the beginning of this chapter using the answer guidelines below.

☐ Go to the **companion website** to access more revision support online, including interactive quizzes, sample questions with answer guidelines, 'you be the marker' exercises, flashcards and podcasts you can download.

Answer guidelines

See the problem question at the start of this chapter.

Approaching the question

Note carefully exactly what the question asks you to do. Here it asks you to advise on the validity of the gifts. If the gifts are not valid trusts then who gets them? Always find a home for the property! Make it a habit to check at the end of answering a certainties question (and other trusts questions) that you have decided where the property will go to.

Deal with all three certainties when looking at each situation, even if in some cases the answer is so obvious that you do not spend much time on some areas.

Never waste time in dealing with the question of the validity of the will. Do not set out the formalities for a valid will unless the question asks you to do this. Assume that the will is valid and go straight to the certainties issues unless directed otherwise. It would be very unlikely that some issue of the validity of the will would arise in a question like this.

Important points to include

Part (a). 'Safe in the knowledge': this may not satisfy the requirement of certainty of intention. Look at the cases (e.g. *Re Adams and Kensington Vestry*) and decide if it indicates the imposition of a trust. If there is no trust there will be an absolute gift to John.

Part (b). There is probably certainty of intention: 'provided that', although this should be discussed. The problem is that there appears to be no certainty of subject matter unless the principle in *Re Golay* applies and external evidence can establish what a reasonable sum is – the words 'a few of the little comforts of life' may help here. If no trust, then the whole sum will go to Barbara.

Part (c). Can the *Re Barlow* principle apply? This seems to be a conditional gift as being a friend is a condition of selecting a book. If so, then provided that the court is prepared to lay down conditions for friendship the gift will be valid.

Part (d). There is no doubt of certainty of intention and subject matter (but gain a few marks by just pointing this out) but is there certainty of objects? A close look at *McPhail* v *Doulton* is needed here, as this is a discretionary trust. Mention and apply the distinction between evidential and conceptual uncertainty. Probably valid. If not, a resulting trust for Susan's estate.

 Make your answer stand out

Analyse the situation in (c) very carefully and explain the decision in *Re Barlow* and any problems associated with it very clearly.

READ TO IMPRESS

Emery, C. (1982) 'The Most Hallowed Principle', 98 LQR 551.

Harris, J. (1971) 'Trust, Power and Duty', 87 LQR 31. This analyses the decision in *McPhail* v *Doulton*.

Hayton, D. (1994) 'Uncertainty of Subject Matter of Trusts', 110 LQR 335.

NOTES

The beneficiary principle and purpose trusts

Revision checklist

Essential points you should know:

☐ why non-charitable purpose trusts are generally held void

☐ the special rules on trusts for animals and monuments and the principle in *Re Denley*

☐ what the rules against perpetuities are (in brief) and how they affect these trusts

☐ what an unincorporated association is and why gifts to them cause problems

☐ the possible solutions: trust for members or gift to the members on a contractual basis

☐ the ways of disposing of surplus funds of unincorporated associations

■ Topic map

General rule: these
trusts are void

Reasons why they
are void

Exceptional cases where trusts for
non-charitable purposes are valid:
- Animals
- Monuments
- Re *Denley* type

Effect of the
perpetuity rules

Gifts are unincorporated associations:
- What are the problems?
- Possible solutions?

A printable version of this topic map is available from **www.pearsoned.co.uk/lawexpress**

■Introduction

The fact that this is a complex area should not put you off answering a question on it because examiners, knowing that the topic is complex, will reward candidates who make a decent attempt at the question.

You should not attempt a question on this area without a good knowledge of charitable trusts, as your answer will require you to explain why the trust is not charitable, which is why it falls into this category.

ASSESSMENT ADVICE

Essay questions An essay question will almost certainly focus on the reasons why non-charitable purpose trusts are generally held to be void and so you will need not only a good knowledge of the law but also of thinking in this area.

Problem questions A problem question may involve one or more gifts and ask you to decide if they are valid. You will need to explain why they are not valid charitable gifts, although this should not occupy too much of your time as the question is not a charity one. You may decide to investigate if the gift could take effect as a valid private trust and here you will need to investigate if it satisfies the rules on certainty of objects (see Chapter 3). This is well worth doing as it shows the examiner that you are thinking laterally, although only do so if there is a reasonable possibility of a valid private trust. The other possibility is that it may be a gift to an unincorporated association in which case the law is the same as for other non-charitable purpose trusts but will need to be approached from a different angle. In both situations you will also need to mention the application of the rule against perpetuities.

■Sample question

Could you answer this question? Below is a typical problem question that could arise on this topic. Guidelines on answering the question are included at the end of this chapter, while a sample essay question and guidance on tackling it can be found on the companion website.

PROBLEM QUESTION

John wishes to make a will under which:

1 £10,000 is left for the maintenance of his tomb in the churchyard of St Catherine's Church Droitwich
2 £1000 is left for the maintenance of his dog, Hugo
3 £20,000 is left to the Hanbury Cricket Club to build a new pavilion
4 £50,000 is left to the Worcester Branch of the XYZ Political Party.

Can you advise John on whether and to what extent his wishes can be carried out?

■ General rule for non-charitable purpose trusts

The general rule is that these trusts are void.

KEY CASE

Re Astor's Settlement Trusts [1952] Ch 534 (HC)

Concerning: non-charitable purpose trusts

Facts

A trust was established for various purposes including the maintenance of good relations between nations and the preservation of the independence of newspapers.

Legal principle

The trust was void. It was for non-charitable purposes (it was not even argued that they were charitable) and there was no one who could enforce the trust.

REVISION NOTE

Go to Chapter 10 and see why these purposes were not charitable.

This was the first time that the courts clearly held that these trusts were void. Why was this so? The best way is to set these trusts in the context of trusts in general (see Figure 4.1).

Figure 4.1

You need to remember that Figure 4.1 is only a sketch and that various details need to be fitted in but it should guide you through this area.

Reasons why these trusts are void

Look at Figure 4.1 and consider the following two points:

1 A trust must have someone who can compel performance of it (the beneficiary principle).
2 The origin of this principle is in a statement of Grant MR in *Morice* v *Bishop of Durham* (1805).

How do the trusts in Figure 4.1 fare?

■ A private trust can be enforced by the beneficiaries

■ A charitable trust can be enforced by the Attorney General

■ A non-charitable purpose trust has no one to enforce it.

The objects of a trust (except a charitable trust) must be expressed with sufficient certainty to enable the court to control it. This is really another way of looking at the issue raised by the beneficiary principle: the need for the court to be able to control the trust.

If the objects of the trust in *Re Astor* were not carried out, who would be able to take action? Even if there was someone to argue in court that there was a breach of these trusts, could the court tell if this was so? If all the trust funds in *Re Astor* were being spent on the promotion of war instead of peace then the court could no doubt find a breach but look at some of the other cases below and see if the court could decide if there was a breach.

The principle in *Re Astor* has been applied to:

■ a trust for the purposes of a contemplative order of nuns (*Leahy* v *A-G for New South Wales* [1959]).

■ a trust for the Labour Party (*Re Grant's Will Trusts* [1979])
■ a trust to provide a useful memorial (*Re Endacott* [1960]).

In the rest of this chapter we shall refer to the *Re Astor* principle as the 'beneficiary principle'.

 Make your answer stand out

See Chapter 1 of *Trends in Contemporary Trust Law* (Matthews, 1996). If you are aiming for an above average mark on this question then you must read further than the textbooks on the issues involved here and this chapter is the place to start.

The way forward is now to look at:

■ ways in which the courts have tried to limit the scope of the beneficiary principle
■ ways in which the beneficiary principle comes into conflict with other rules and concepts
■ ways in which the law might develop in the future.

Return to Figure 4.1. You will see that it mentions two situations where these trusts may be valid and you need to consider them in more detail.

■ Exceptions to the beneficiary principle

Trusts to care for animals and for the upkeep of specific monuments

This is an anomaly. Remember that *Re Astor* was the first case where the beneficiary principle was held to invalidate trusts for non-charitable purposes. Thus before then, although it was realised that there were objections to them, there was some freedom for the courts to develop the law as they saw fit. This explains this exception.

Some cases are *Re Hooper* [1932] (monuments) and *Re Dean* (1889) (animals).

Note that the courts now confine these cases within narrow limits: for example, a gift to maintain an animal and also to breed from it would not be valid – breeding would take it beyond caring. This is a common examination point.

Note also *Re Endacott* [1960]: an example of the unwillingness of the courts to extend the law here.

Trusts of the *Re Denley* type

KEY CASE

Re Denley's Trust Deed [1969] 1 Ch 373 (HC)
Concerning: validity of a trust which appeared to be primarily for purposes and not persons

Facts

Land was conveyed to trustees to hold it for the purpose of a recreation or sports ground primarily for the benefit of the employees of a company and then for the benefit of such other person(s) as the trustees might allow.

Legal principle

The trust was valid as it was for the benefit of the employees and it was not a purpose trust.

EXAM TIP

Examiners will expect you to be able to analyse the issues in this case so be prepared and read, for example, Everton (1982).

■ Ways in which the beneficiary principle comes into conflict with other rules and concepts

Having learnt the rule and the exceptions to the beneficiary principle you now need to be able to appreciate how it comes into collision with two other areas: the perpetuity rules and gifts to unincorporated associations (see Figure 4.2).

Figure 4.2

Principle that a trust for non-charitable purposes is void

Also involves

Rule against perpetuities   Law on unincorporated associations

Effect of the perpetuity rules

Example 4.1

John leaves £1000 to Tim on trust to care for the monument over his tombstone. When is the trust to end? When Tim dies it is possible for new trustees to be appointed but this is not the point. When will the trust end?

The law feels that non-charitable purpose trusts should have a lifespan. The **rule against perpetuities** fixes this.

KEY DEFINITION: Perpetuity rule

Section 5 of the Perpetuities and Accumulations Act 2009 (which comes into force on a date to be appointed in 2010) provides for a period of 125 years which overrides any different provision in the trust instrument. The 'wait and see' provisions are preserved by s. 7. However, s. 16 of this Act inserts a new s. 5A into the Perpetuities and Accumulations Act 1964 which provides that the new period will not apply to a will (but will apply to other documents) executed before the 2009 Act comes into force. In this case s. 15(4) of 1964 Act will apply and this provides that a gift to be held for a non-charitable purpose trust is void if it may last beyond lives or lives in being plus 21 years.

EXAM TIP

If a question involves a purpose trust contained in a will check when the will was executed.

In fact, the courts have tried to ensure that these trusts do not fall foul of the perpetuity period. See *Mussett* v *Bingle* (1876) regarding the assumption that a monument would be erected within the perpetuity period.

Note: *Re Haines* (1952); the courts take notice of the lifespan of particular animals. Here that a cat could not live longer than 21 years. Thus the gift was valid.

Where a trust states that it is to last for 'as long as the law allows' this will be taken to be the perpetuity period and so it will be valid (*Re Hooper* (1932)).

Gifts to unincorporated associations

! Don't be tempted to...

Don't skip over the topic of validity of gifts to unincorporated associations! This can be a difficult area in problem questions as it involves the following three areas:

1 beneficiary principle
2 rule against perpetuities
3 nature of unincorporated associations.

Do keep each point distinct and apply separately to the question.

The fundamental point is that unincorporated associations do not exist in law and so any gift must be for their purposes.

Although Barbara (below) may think she has made a gift to the club itself, she has not.

REVISION NOTE

Go to Chapter 10 and check that you are clear on the law on the disposal of the surplus funds of unincorporated associations.

Example 4.2

Figure 4.3

Although Barbara may think she has made a gift to the club itself, she has not. Assuming that it is not a registered company, the club is an unincorporated association and so does not exist.

The next question is whether the club can be a charity.

Under the Charities Act 2006 if the club is amateur the gift can be for charitable purposes and be valid.

Let us assume that the Hanbury FC is semi-professional. Here we have a problem as the gift is for non-charitable purposes and must be held on trust, but these trusts are void. The same would apply if the gift had been made to a political party.

 Make your answer stand out

The fact that there are legal difficulties with these gifts has caused adverse comment. A good example is:

'It would astonish a layman to be told that there was a difficulty in his giving a legacy to an unincorporated non-charitable society which he had or could have supported without difficulty in his lifetime'. (Brightman J in *Re Recher's Will Trusts* [1972])

The result is that the courts have tried to find ways of making these gifts valid. There are two possibilities:

1 a gift on trust for the benefit of the members – see *Re Denley* above
2 a gift to the members who will hold it on the basis of the contract between them contained in the rules of the association – see *Re Recher* below.

These possibilities often form part of a problem question in an exam. We need now to look at them carefully.

KEY CASE

Re Recher's Will Trusts [1972] Ch 526 (HC)
Concerning: validity of gifts to unincorporated associations

Facts

A gift was made to the London and Provincial Anti-Vivisection Society, a non-charitable association.

Legal principle

This was valid as it was a gift to the members as an addition to the funds subject to the contract between them as set out in the rules. It was not an immediate gift to the members.

Compare this with *Re Lipinski's Will Trusts* (1976).

KEY CASE

Re Horley Town Football Club; Hunt v *McLaren* (2006) EWHC 2386 (HC)
Concerning: validity of gifts to unincorporated associations

Facts

The club was an unincorporated association. In 1948 the then president of the club had settled land on trust to secure a permanent endowment for the club and in 2002 the land was sold and the proceeds used to buy other land and provide sports facilities. A surplus remained and the issue was the precise basis on which the assets of the club were held.

Legal principle

The trust deed of 1948 should be interpreted as a gift to the club as a contract-holding gift to the club members for the time being. The beneficial interest vested in the current full members and was held on a bare trust for them. This entitled them to call in a general meeting for the assets to be transferred to them as individuals. The decision follows *Re Recher* in basing the solution on contract but the device of a trust is used to solve the problem of exactly where the legal ownership of the property lies pending any distribution between the members.

 Make your answer stand out

There have not been many recent cases on this area and so a good knowledge of the above case will obviously bring extra marks in an exam. Research it! A good place to start is Luxton (2007).

But there is still a problem: the **rule against perpetuities**:

KEY CASE

Re Grant's Will Trusts **[1979] 3 All ER 359 (HC)**

Concerning: application of the Rule against Perpetuities to gifts to unincorporated non-charitable bodies

Facts

A gift was made for the purposes of the Chertsey Labour Party but the members did not control the property nor could they gain control as the rules were subject to the jurisdiction of the National Executive of the Labour Party.

Legal principle

A gift to a non-charitable unincorporated association will fail if the members are unable to divide the gift between them, as it will have to be held for the association's purposes in perpetuity.

In *Re Horley Town Football Club* (above) the actual trust deed did define a perpetuity period but perpetuity was not a problem as the interests of the members vested immediately.

Note: Another area where the apparent lack of a beneficiary could cause problems with the enforcement of a trust (although so far it seems not to have done so) is the Quistclose type of trust dealt with in Chapter 8. This is discussed in the article by Pawlowski and Summers (2007: 445).

Future development of the law

✓ Make your answer stand out

As essay questions are likely in this area it is absolutely vital that you read widely and think about the issues. Look at the idea of these trusts having an enforcer who will be able to take action to enforce the trust. This would solve the fundamental problem posed at the start of this chapter. See Warburton (1985) and Pawlowski and Summers (2007). The latter argue for a general recognition by English Law of the validity of non-charitable purpose trusts provided that certain conditions are satisfied, in particular, that an enforcer is named in the trust instrument who is independent of the settlor and the beneficiaries.

■Chapter summary: putting it all together

Test yourself

☐ Can you tick all the points from the **revision checklist** at the beginning of this chapter?

☐ Attempt the **sample question** from the beginning of this chapter using the answer guidelines below.

☐ Go to the **companion website** to access more revision support online, including interactive quizzes, sample questions with answer guidelines, 'you be the marker' exercises, flashcards and podcasts you can download.

Answer guidelines

See the problem question at the start of this chapter.

Approaching the question

This question requires a clear knowledge of gifts which may be invalid as non-charitable purpose trusts together with the ability to recognise and apply the perpetuity rules.

Important points to include

1 Maintenance of tomb: valid in principle but note the perpetuity point. Apply the Perpetuities and Accumulations Act 2009. Apply the perpetuity period and also 'wait and see'.

2 Possibly valid as it is for the upkeep of a specific animal and not to breed from it. Is it void as a perpetuity though?

3 Can it be a trust for the benefit of the club members (*Re Denley*)? Or a gift to the members to be held on the basis of the contract between them (*Re Recher*)? Note the similarity with *Re Lipinski*.

4 Similar issues to those in (c) but as the money is not allocated to a specific purpose there is the possibility that it may infringe the rule against perpetuities. Can the members divide the gift among themselves or are they subject to control by the political party? See *Re Grant*.

▶

Make your answer stand out

Apply the rules in this chapter but also:

■ explain the perpetuities rule clearly

■ sketch in the underlying points: the beneficiary principle and the fact that in (c) and (d) these are unincorporated associations.

■ could the gift in 3 be charitable?

READ TO IMPRESS

Brown, J. (2007) 'What are we to do with Testamentary Trusts of Imperfect Obligation?', 71 Conv. 148.

Everton, A. (1982) Conv. 118.

Luxton, P. (2007) *Re Horley Town Football Club*, 71 Conv. 274.

Matthews, P. (1996) 'The New Trust: Obligations without Rights?' in *Trends in Contemporary Trust Law* ed. A. Oakley, Oxford: Oxford University Press.

Pawlowski, M. and Summers, P. (2007) 'Private Purpose Trusts – a Reform Proposal', 71 Conv. 445.

Warburton, J. (1985) 'Holding of Property by Unincorporated Associations', Conv. 318.

NOTES

NOTES

NOTES

Formalities

5

Revision checklist

Essential points you should know:

☐ the formalities when a trust of land is declared
☐ the formalities when an equitable interest under any trust is transferred
☐ the failure to observe these formalities: what the consequences are

■ Topic map

■Introduction

The basic principles of formalties are reasonably straightforward and the number of variations on them is not great.

A good attempt at a problem on formalities will be well rewarded. In addition the subject provides excellent material for essay questions.

Remember also that in order to be valid, a trust must not only comply with any requisite formalities, it must also comply with the three certainties. Check Chapter 3 and make sure that you can recall the three certainties.

ASSESSMENT ADVICE

Essay questions Essays in this area will require you to have read and mastered the detail of the complex cases such as *Oughtred* v *IRC* (1960) and *Vandervell* v *IRC* (1967), and looked at the justification for these rules. You may also have a question on other areas such as constitution of a trust where you will need to deal with this area.

Problem questions These will usually deal with a variety of situations and ask you whether the statutory provisions on the formalities will apply and, if so, what the effect of non-observance will be. Draw a diagram of the situations and remember that these types of problem questions are asking you for a sound, logical approach. Spend time before writing to get your ideas in order.

■Sample question

Could you answer this question? Below is a typical problem question that could arise on this topic. Guidelines on answering the question are included at the end of this chapter, while a sample essay question and guidance on tackling it can be found on the companion website.

PROBLEM QUESTION

Isabel owns a house 'The Gables' and also has £20,000 in an account at the Worcester Bank. In addition she is the beneficiary under a trust fund consisting of 1000 shares in ABC Co. Ltd, set up for her by her late father Albert, of which her brother Frank is now the trustee. She says to her son, Larry: 'In future I will hold 'The Gables' for you but it will still stay in my name. The same applies to the money in the Worcester Bank.' She then rings Frank and says, 'I really do not need those shares in the ABC Co. anymore. In future pay any dividends to Larry.'

The next day Isabel dies and Hubert, her **executor**, asks your advice on whether and to what extent 'The Gables', the £20,000 in the bank account and the shares in the ABC Co. Ltd form part of Isabel's estate.

■ Declaration of a trust of land

KEY STATUTE

Law of Property Act 1925, s. 53(1)(b)

'A declaration of trust concerning land or any interest therein must be manifested and proved by some writing signed by some person who is able to declare the same or by his will.'

Example 5.1

Claud is the owner of a house known as 'The Laurels' and says to some friends: 'From now on I am holding 'The Laurels' in trust for my children Tom and Tim'. This is not enforceable, as there is nothing in writing.

Points to note:

■ The actual declaration of trust need not be in writing. The words 'manifested and proved' require only written evidence of the details of the trust and do not require that the actual trust should be in writing. Therefore evidence can be, for example, in two or more documents which are linked.

■ The signature of the settlor is probably needed. The words in s. 53(1)(b) are 'signed by some person who is able to declare the same' and this is generally taken to mean that an agent cannot sign although the point has never been decided.

■ The requirement in s. 53(1)(b) applies only to express trusts and not to resulting, implied or constructive trusts (s. 53 (2)). This exception is of great importance as it has enabled the courts to impose a resulting, implied or constructive trust in many cases where there was no written declaration of trust.

> **REVISION NOTE**
>
> Good examples of s. 53(2) are those involving disputes over the beneficial entitlement to the family home and where it is felt necessary to impose a trust to prevent fraud or unconscionable conduct (see Chapter 9 and below).

■ No formalities are required for *inter vivos* declarations of trusts of other property. Where the trust is created by will there are statutory requirements but these will not be relevant for a trusts exam as wills fall within the law of succession.

Note the distinction between the formalities requirements and constitution of a trust (Chapter 6). Constitution deals with the actual transfer of the trust property but here we are concerned with a preliminary issue: Did the actual declaration of a trust observe the required formalities?

Failure to observe the requirements of s. 53(1)(b)

Section 53(1)(b) itself is silent on the position when these requirements are not complied with but it is accepted that this will not make the trust void but only unenforceable (*Gardner* v *Rowe* (1828)). *Void* means that the trust is of no effect at all. *Unenforceable* means that, although the trust is valid, it cannot be enforced in any legal proceedings.

However, in the case below, the court held that a trust could be imposed where the effect of the operation of s. 53(1)(b) would be to permit fraud.

> **KEY CASE**
>
> *Rochefoucauld* v *Boustead* [1897] 1 Ch 196 (CA)
>
> *Concerning: whether a formality requirement should be set aside as it is an instrument of fraud*
>
> **Facts**
>
> The claimant had mortgaged land but was having difficulty in repaying the mortgage. The defendant bought the land and orally agreed to hold it as trustee for the claimant. However, he treated the land as his own.   ▶

Legal principle

The claimant was entitled to an account of profits made on the land because although the trust was in the claimant's favour, not being in writing it did not satisfy the requirements of what is now s. 53(1)(b), LPA 1925. It would thus be a fraud on the defendant's part to take the profits for himself.

 Make your answer stand out

This case is sometimes used as an example of the operation of constructive trusts as the 'instrument of fraud' principle is usually found in that context. You will gain marks for pointing out that here an express trust was imposed but you should point out that in other cases the courts have thought that a resulting or a constructive trust was more appropriate and, of course, these trusts are exempted from the formality requirement of s. 53(1)(b) by s. 53(2) (above). An instance of this is *Hodgson* v *Marks* (1971) (see Chapter 8) and see also Chapter 9.

■ Dispositions of equitable interests arising under trusts

It is vital to be absolutely clear about when this happens by contrast with a declaration of trust which was dealt with above. One simple way is this:

■ Section 53(1)(b) applies when a trust is being declared

■ Section 53(1)(c) applies when the trust is up and running but it is intended to move interests of beneficiaries under it (i.e. equitable interests) from one person to another.

Note that these two subsections operate at different stages (see Figure 5.1).

KEY STATUTE

Law of Property Act 1925, s. 53(1)(c)

A disposition of an equitable interest or trust must be in writing signed either by the settlor or by his authorised agent.

Figure 5.1

John declares in writing that his house 'Equity' is now held by Bernard in trust for Miranda

John
(Settlor)
⟶
Bernard
(Trustee)

(s. 53(1)(b) is complied with)

Jason
(Beneficiary)
⟵
Miranda

Miranda by writing transfers her interest in 'Equity' to Jason

(s. 53(1)(c) is complied with)

Points to note:

- The actual disposition must be in writing. Written evidence will not suffice
- The signature of an agent is sufficient
- Section 53(1)(c) does not, by virtue of s. 53(2), apply to resulting, implied or constructive trusts
- Where a disposition of an equitable interest is made which is to be held on trust, then although the actual disposition must be in writing, the details of the trust need not be (*Re Tyler's Fund Trusts* (1967))
- There is no requirement for the trustees to be notified of the disposition – a useful point to add in an exam answer.

Application of s. 53(1)(c)

An exam question will deal with situations where the application of s. 53(1)(c) has been considered by the courts. We will now look at each of these but before we do, you may find the following quote from Moffat (2009: 135) useful: 'if at the commencement of a transaction a person has a subsisting equitable interest and at the end no longer has that interest, then there has been a disposition within s. 53(1)(c)'.

The reason why many of the cases discussed in this chapter were brought was that settlors have tried to avoid payment of stamp duty which is payable on the written instrument by which property is transferred, but many settlors have argued that as a particular transaction is not a disposition within the meaning of s. 53(1)(c), no writing is needed and therefore no stamp duty is payable.

In the following examples, T holds on trust for X absolutely. T is the trustee and X is the beneficiary.

Transfer by beneficiary (X) of her equitable interest to another

Figure 5.2

X transfers her interest to Y

In Figure 5.2 writing is obviously needed.

Direction to a beneficiary (X) to trustees that they are now to hold on trust for another person

Figure 5.3 shows an example.

Figure 5.3

X directs T to hold the property on trust for Y

KEY CASE

Grey v *IRC* **[1960] AC 1 (HL)**

Concerning: whether a direction by a beneficiary to trustees to hold the trust property on trust for another is a disposition within s. 53 (1)(c)

Facts

The settlor transferred shares to trustees to hold as nominees for him. He then orally (i.e. no writing) directed the trustees to hold the shares on trust for his grandchildren and the trustees later executed a written declaration of trust.

Legal principle

A direction by a beneficiary to trustees to hold on trust for another is a disposition within s. 53(1)(c).

Transfer of the legal estate by a bare trustee to another

KEY DEFINITION: Bare trustee

A bare trustee is a trustee with no active duties and so can be given directions by the beneficiary to transfer the legal estate.

Example 5.2

X (beneficiary) directs T to transfer shares to Y so that Y becomes the absolute owner. A possible form of words could be: 'All my interest in the shares is to go to Y.' The word 'all' could mean that not only the equitable interest in the shares, which belongs to X, but also the legal title to them, which is held by T, should go to Y.

KEY CASE

Vandervell v *IRC* [1967] 2 AC 291 (HL)

Concerning: whether a transfer of the legal estate, where there is an existing equitable interest, to another requires writing under s. 53(1)(c)

Facts

A bank which held shares for Vandervell as a **bare trustee** transferred them, on his directions, to the Royal College of Surgeons subject to an option exercisable by Vandervell Trustees Ltd to repurchase the shares. The bank's legal title to the shares and Vandervell's equitable interest in them were accordingly both transferred and it was held that this transaction was not caught by s. 53(1)(c) and so writing was not needed.

Legal principle

A transfer of the legal estate to another does not require writing.

Although the equitable interest passes from X to Y this is done automatically with the transfer of the legal estate and thus there is no separate disposition.

New trusts are declared by the trustee with the consent of the beneficiary

Example 5.3

T declares, with the agreement of X, that he now holds the property on trust for W.

KEY CASE

Re Vandervell's Trusts (No. 2) [1974] Ch 269 (CA)

Concerning: declaration of new trusts

Facts

Following from the decision in *Vandervell* v *IRC* (above) Vandervell instructed Vandervell Trustees to exercise the option to repurchase the shares which were intended to be held on the trusts of the Vandervell children's settlement.

Legal principle

It was held that where new trusts are declared with the consent of the beneficiary then this was not within s. 53(1)(c) so writing was not required.

Make your answer stand out

Refer to Green (1984) who critically reviews the case law, especially the Vandervell cases.

Beneficiary contracts to transfer his equitable interest

Example 5.4

X contracts with Z to transfer his interest under the trust to him.

The law here awaits clarification and the leading case is:

KEY CASE

Oughtred v *IRC* [1960] AC 206 (HL)

Concerning: whether a contract to transfer a beneficial interest under a trust is caught by s. 53(1)(c)

Facts

X and Y had separate interests in shares in a private company. They orally agreed to exchange their interests and the IRC claimed stamp duty on the actual written transfer of the shares.

Legal principle

In the case of a contract to sell shares in a private company the remedy of specific performance is available because the shares are unique and so a constructive trust arises in favour of the buyer. The buyer does not acquire a full beneficial interest until the formal written transfer. This is therefore the disposition and s. 53(1)(c) applies to it. Lord Radcliffe, however, dissented and held that Mrs Oughtred obtained the ownership in equity by virtue of the agreement and this view has been supported by later cases (see *Re Hay* [1982]).

 Make your answer stand out

Note that a later case to deal with the matter in depth, *Neville* v *Wilson* [1997] supports Lord Radcliffe's argument (see Figure 5.4). See, for a discussion of this case, Milne (1997).

Figure 5.4

The sequence of events in the example based on Lord Radcliffe's dissent in
Oughtred v *IRC* is:

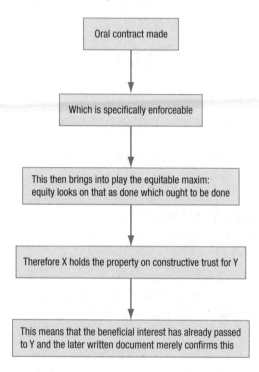

Oral contract made

Which is specifically enforceable

This then brings into play the equitable maxim:
equity looks on that as done which ought to be done

Therefore X holds the property on constructive trust for Y

This means that the beneficial interest has already passed
to Y and the later written document merely confirms this

Beneficiary declares herself trustee

As a sub-trust has been created (Figure 5.5), it can be argued that this is a declaration
of trust and so it falls within s. 53(1)(b), in which case writing is only needed if
it concerns land. However, if X has no active duties to perform and is thus a bare
trustee then the effect is that X will have disappeared from the picture and there may
be a disposition from X to Y.

Figure 5.5

X declares that she now holds the property as trustee for Y

T

X

(Beneficiary as regards T but a trustee for Y)

Y

Beneficiary surrenders her equitable interest

Example 5.5

X surrenders her interest to T1 and T2.

The position is uncertain but it could be argued, by analogy with *Vandervell* v *IRC* (above) that as the legal and equitable titles are now merged there is no disposition.

Beneficiary disclaims her equitable interest

Example 5.6

X, as soon as she becomes aware that she has an equitable interest, disclaims it.

KEY CASE

Re Paradise Motor Co. Ltd **[1968] 1 WLR 1125 (HC)**
Concerning: disclaimer of an equitable interest

Facts
The facts were the same as in the example.

Legal principle
Writing is not needed here because 'a disclaimer operates by way of avoidance and not by way of disposition' (Danckwerts LJ).

Beneficiary under a staff pension fund appoints a nominee to receive benefits from the fund

Example 5.7

X, a beneficiary under a staff pension fund, appoints T to receive the money payable by the fund in the event of X's death.

KEY CASE

Re Danish Bacon Co. Ltd Staff Pension Fund [1971] 1 WLR 248 (HC)

Concerning: nominations of benefits in a pension fund

Facts

An employee had nominated his wife to receive benefits payable to him under a pension fund and had then, by a separate letter, changed his mind.

Legal principle

Megarry J doubted if this was a disposition requiring writing, but, if it was, the writing was supplied by connecting the two documents.

Failure to comply with the requirements of s. 53(1)(c)

The result is that the disposition is void.

■ Why formalities are needed

To prevent fraud. This is the rationale for s. 53(1)(c).

Example 5.8

John says that Susan has declared that she now holds her house on trust for him. Susan denies this. The only way in which John can prove this is by producing written evidence. This is the same principle as the requirement of writing in an actual contract for the sale of land.

- To enable the trustees to know what is going on. This is the rationale for s. 53(1)(c).

Example 5.9

Gerald is a trustee of property for Jane. Jane tells Gerald that she has transferred her interest to Mark and in future Gerald should treat Mark as the beneficiary. What if Jane is wrong? Gerald must require writing to prove that Jane's beneficial interest has been transferred to Mark.

✓ Make your answer stand out

The complexity of this area has led to calls for reform. The Law Commission proposed to issue a Consultation Paper in 1999 which could have led to legislation but due to work on other projects it was put back and there is no date for any proposals. Look at Battersby (1979) for a critique of the law.

■Chapter summary: putting it all together

Test yourself

☐ Can you tick all the points from the **revision checklist** at the beginning of this chapter?

☐ Attempt the **sample question** from the beginning of this chapter using the answer guidelines below.

☐ Go to the **companion website** to access more revision support online, including interactive quizzes, sample questions with answer guidelines, 'you be the marker' exercises, flashcards and podcasts you can download.

Answer guidelines

See the problem question at the start of this chapter.

Approaching the question

Begin by explaining why Hubert's question is important. If Isabel has really divested herself of any interest in the property then it will no longer form part of her estate. Then look at each point in turn.

Important points to include

■ The Gables: This appears to be an attempt to declare a trust of land but *your marks will be increased* if you discuss whether this is a declaration of trust anyway. Isabel has not actually used the word 'trust' here so you can make use of your knowledge of certainty of intention to create a trust (see Chapter 3).

■ Assuming that it is a declaration of trust, then does it comply with the requirements of s. 53(1)(b) LPA 1925? Clearly not as it is not in writing or evidenced by writing. So the declaration is not void but cannot be enforced against Isabel's estate.

■ £20,000 in the bank account. The same points apply here as well: is there an actual declaration of trust? If it is then it is valid as s. 53(1)(b) only applies to land.

■ Shares in the ABC Co.: Isabel is a beneficiary here and she is attempting to dispose of her equitable interest under the trust. Again, extra marks for spotting that she has not actually used the words 'dispose of my equitable interest' but this is what she has actually done. Refer to s. 53(1)(c) and note that it requires writing. This case is similar to *Grey* v *IRC* in that the beneficiary has directed the trustee to hold the property for another rather than make a direct disposition but applying *Grey* v *IRC* it is still caught by s. 53(1)(c). Therefore as she has not used writing it is void and so Isabel's estate is still a beneficiary of the shares.

 Make your answer stand out

Show that you have:

■ a thorough knowledge of the law which is clearly applied

■ paid close attention to the actual words of the relevant sections of the LPA

■ knowledge of the reasons why formalities are required – a mention of this would impress the examiner in an answer to a problem question.

READ TO IMPRESS

Battersby, G. (1979) 'Formalities for the Disposition of Equitable Interests under Trusts', 43 *Conv.* 17 at 38.

Green, B. (1984) 'Grey, Oughtred and Vandervell – A Contextual Re Appraisal', 47 MLR 385.

Milne, P. (1997) 'Oughtred Revisted', 113 LQR 213.

Moffat, G. (2009) *Trusts Law and Materials*, p. 135, 5th edn, Cambridge: Cambridge University Press.

Nolan, R. (1996) 'The Triumph of Technicality', 55 CLJ 436.

NOTES

NOTES

Constitution

Revision checklist

Essential points you should know:

- [ ] the methods of constituting a trust
- [ ] the principle in *Re Rose* and its application in more recent cases
- [ ] the position of beneficiaries and trustees where the trust is incompletely constituted
- [ ] indirect constitution as in *Re Ralli*
- [ ] the three ways in which equity may assist a volunteer

Topic map

■Introduction

Constitution of trusts is one of the major areas of equity and trusts and is likely to attract a question.

It can be one on its own or the question can be combined with either or both certainties or formalities and so you should always revise these areas carefully. There have been two fairly recent cases, *Choithram (T) International SA* v *Pagarani* [2001] and *Pennington* v *Waine* [2002] which are obviously likely to inspire questions. Note that two topics may only be dealt with in outline in an equity course as they may appear in other subjects: *Donationes mortis causa* (succession) and *Estoppel* (land law).

ASSESSMENT ADVICE

Essay questions A familiar essay question asks you to comment on the equitable maxim 'equity will not assist a volunteer' in the light of the law on constitution. Another could ask about the effect of *Pennington* v *Waine* [2002] on the requirements for constitution or deal with particular areas such as the three cases where equity may assist a volunteer.

Problem questions Problem questions often involve a range of situations and ask you to decide if the trust has been completely constituted in each. This is a good area for picking up marks as there will be a wide range of issues and you ought to be able to say something useful on at least some of them! In many questions the person attempting the transfer (X) will have died and so the contest will be between the trustee/beneficiary who will be claiming that the trust was properly constituted and the person (Y) who was left the property under the will of X. Y will, of course, claim that the trust was incompletely constituted and so it still formed part of X's estate when he died and so passes to them. Do make a note of who Y is at the start of your answer and, as ever, always find a home for the property: do not leave it unallocated.

When answering a problem question identify, in relation to each piece of property, what formalities were required to validly transfer it and if they have been complied with. If not, then consider if any of the exceptions outlined below apply.

■ Sample question

Could you answer this question? Below is a typical problem question that could arise on this topic. Guidelines on answering the question are included at the end of this chapter, while a sample essay question and guidance on tackling it can be found on the companion website.

PROBLEM QUESTION

Joshua suffered a haemorrhage and was rushed to hospital. His niece, Belinda, his son, Charles, his daughter, Fiona, and his friend, Laura, all visited him.

He said to Belinda: 'Here are the deeds to my house 'Laurels'. As you know, I have always intended you to have it and now it is yours.'

He asked Charles to bring him the lease to his shop and he wrote on it: 'I now declare that the benefit of this shop belongs to Charles absolutely.'

He told Fiona: 'You have been wonderful to me. You gave up your job to look after me and it was always understood between us that you would be rewarded. My seaside cottage is now yours.'

He said to Laura: 'I am not long for this world. Here is my post office savings book. This account is now yours. I have made out the necessary forms to put it into your name – here they are.'

That night Joshua died when the hospital was struck by lightning. His will appointed Fiona as his executrix.

Can you advise Belinda, Charles, Fiona and Laura as to any claims they might have to Joshua's property? Would it make any difference to your answer if Joshua had died six months later when playing tennis from an undetected heart condition?

■ Ways in which a trust can be constituted

Before looking at constitution, note the distinction between constitution and formalities, which was dealt with in Chapter 5. Questions may deal with both of these.

Look at these situations:

Example 6.1

Situation one	Situation two
Fred transfers £1000 into a trust account in the name of his two trustees (Tim and Ted) to be held on the terms of a trust which he has declared for his two children, Mark and Charlotte.	Fred promises Tim and Ted that he will transfer £1000 into the trust account for Mark and Charlotte but fails to do so.

The difference is obvious: in the first situation Fred has transferred the money into the names of his trustees and so it is no longer Fred's money; in the second Fred has promised to do so but no transfer has taken place.

In situation one the trust is said to be **constituted** but in situation two it is not.

KEY DEFINITION: Constitution of a trust

A trust is *constituted* when the legal title to the trust property is vested in the trustee(s).

A trust is *unconstituted* when the legal title to the trust property is not vested in the trustee(s).

EXAM TIP

Always begin your answer to a problem question on constitution by identifying whether constitution has taken place. It almost certainly will not have done so and so you will then be able to continue by deciding if there is any way in which the trust can be constituted.

Take situation two. The trust has not been constituted. What, if anything, can Mark and Charlotte do?

Your starting point must be the maxim that 'Equity will not assist a volunteer' (e.g. see Lord Eldon in *Ellison* v *Ellison* (1802)).

A person who has not provided any consideration for a promise.

(Note that in equity the term consideration is wider than in the common law of contract.)

Are Mark and Charlotte volunteers? Yes, as there is no evidence of their having provided consideration for Fred's promise to transfer £1000 to Tim and Tom for their benefit.

The point that equity will not assist volunteers is not the end of the matter but is a good and clear way to start!

Figure 6.1

Methods of constituting a trust

The authority for the two methods shown in Figure 6.1 is in the judgment of Turner LJ in *Milroy* v *Lord* (1862).

We will deal with Method one now so as to concentrate on Method two later.

Method one: declaration of settlor as trustee

Example 6.2

Jason has £1000 in a bank account and says to his son, Christopher: 'I am now the trustee of this money for you.'

The effect is that a trust has been set up with Jason as trustee and Christopher as beneficiary (see Figure 6.2).

Figure 6.2

Jason
(Settlor but also trustee when he has declared the trust)

Christopher (beneficiary)

However, exam questions do not make the scenario as simple as this!

There have been a number of cases on this point and you should note the following carefully:

- *Jones* v *Lock* (1865)
- *Richards* v *Delbridge* (1874)
- *Paul* v *Constance* (1977).

In all of these cases the issue was whether words used by the settlor were enough to make him/her a trustee.

REVISION NOTE

Go back to Chapter 3 and revise intention to create a trust.

The most recent case is as follows:

KEY CASE

Choithram (T) International SA v *Pagarani* [2001] 2 All ER 492 (PC)

Concerning: declaration of self as trustee

Facts

X executed a trust deed which set up a charitable foundation and then said: 'I now give all my wealth to the foundation' (or words to this effect).

Legal principle

This was sufficient to constitute the trust as A was one of the trustees of the foundation and it did not matter that the property had not been vested in the other trustees. In addition, although the words used looked like an outright gift they must have meant that X was constituting a trust.

Make your answer stand out

This decision is controversial. Has it relaxed the law on constitution too much?
Read Hopkins (2001) and Clarke (2001) on this issue.

Method two: transfer to others as trustees

Here there must be three parties (see Figure 6.3).

Figure 6.3

Example 6.3

Take Example 6.2 above. Suppose that Jason had declared himself a trustee, not
of £1000 in his bank account, but of his house.

This is Method one and as this is freehold land, one formality would be needed:

1 The actual declaration of trust would need to be in writing (s. 53(1)(b), LPA 1925
and see Chapter 3).

Suppose that Method two was used and the scenario was:

Example 6.4

Jason intends to transfer his house to Edith to hold on trust for Christopher.

We would now need two formalities:

1 As above, s. 53(1)(b), LPA must be complied with.
2 Section 52(1), LPA which requires transfers of freehold land to be by deed.

Settlor does all in power to constitute the trust (i.e. to transfer the property to the trustees)

Example 6.5

Anne is the owner of 5000 shares in Midland Optical Illusion Co. Ltd, a private company. She wishes to transfer them to her daughter, Susan. However, a private company can refuse to register a transfer.

KEY CASE

Re Rose [1952] Ch 499 (HC)

Concerning: what is needed for the settlor to do all in his power to make the transfer?

Facts

The settlor executed a deed transferring shares in a private company to trustees.

Legal principle

It was enough if the settlor had done everything in his power to make the transfer binding and this was when the deed was executed. Although directors of a private company have a discretion to refuse to register a transfer, at the moment when the deed was executed the settlor had done all in his power to make the transaction binding on him.

This was applied in *Mascall* v *Mascall* (1985) to a transfer of registered land: here it is the Land Registry who completes the transfer.

KEY CASE

Pennington v *Waine* [2002] EWCA Civ 227

Concerning: what is needed to make a transfer binding on a person when another person or body needs to complete the transfer?

Facts

A donor had executed a form transferring shares in a private company to her nephew but had not delivered it to him, instead it had gone to the auditor of the company. The gift was completed, as it was not necessary for the form to be delivered to the nephew.

Legal principle

A gift can be deemed to be complete if it would have been unconscionable for the donor to change their mind at this point.

Make your answer stand out

This case, like *Choithram* (above) is seen as a controversial relaxation of the rules on constitution as the donor did not do all in her power to complete the transfer. Read more on it: see Clarke (2002) and Garton (2003).

Other formal requirements for transfer of property

Other property requires other formalities to transfer it: equitable interests need writing (s. 53(1)(c), LPA 1925; see Chapter 3); and chattels need a deed of gift or the intention to give them or parting with possessions, and shares need the appropriate transfer form and registration of the transferee as owner.

■ Can the beneficiaries compel constitution?

Equity will not assist a volunteer. A volunteer is a person who has not provided consideration. So if the beneficiaries have not provided consideration then equity will not assist them unless the situation is within the three exceptional situations dealt with below. It then becomes crucial to know what is meant by consideration.

Consideration in equity has a wider meaning than at common law because equity also includes marriage consideration.

KEY DEFINITION: Marriage consideration

In equity this includes the husband and wife and the issue of the marriage.

Marriage consideration will appear when a settlement is made either before or after marriage and (this is the crucial point) in consideration of marriage, under which the settlor promises to settle property on his or her (future) husband or wife. If so, they can enforce the promise if it is not carried out and so can their issue (see *Pullan* v *Koe* (1913)). Does it now include a civil partnership?

Suppose that the beneficiaries have not given consideration but they are parties to a deed of covenant under which there is a promise to constitute a trust by settling property on them?

Note that:

■ Equity recognises marriage consideration. Common law does not

■ Common law recognises promises made in a deed (*Cannon* v *Hartley* (1949)). Equity does not

■ Common law remedy is damages. Equitable remedy will probably be specific performance.

In addition the Contracts (Rights of Third Parties) Act 1999 may change the answer.

Take some examples and see how these principles apply to them. Note that for now we are considering whether the beneficiary is able to enforce the promise. We will consider the position of the trustee later.

Assume for now that the Contracts (Rights of Third Parties) Act 1999 does not apply.

Example 6.6

John promises his fiancée Miranda that, in contemplation of his marriage to her he will transfer £10,000 to Robert to hold on trust for her. He fails to do so.

Can Miranda enforce this promise?	Yes
In equity or common law?	Equity – marriage consideration

Therefore equitable remedies, e.g. specific performance (SP).

Example 6.7

John promises Miranda, his girlfriend, that he will transfer £10,000 to Robert on trust for her but fails to do so.

Can Miranda enforce this promise?	No

Miranda is a volunteer – unlike in Example 6.6 there is no evidence of marriage consideration.

Example 6.8

John promises Miranda by a deed to which John, Miranda and Robert are parties that he will transfer £10,000 to Robert to hold on trust for her but fails to do so.

Can Miranda enforce the promise?	Not in equity

Equity does not enforce promises in a deed made without consideration – example of the maxim that equity does not assist a volunteer – Miranda has given no consideration.

However, common law will give a remedy for broken promises in a deed – so Miranda can claim damages.

Contracts (Rights of Third Parties) Act 1999, s. 1

Section 1 enables a person who is not a party to a contract to take the benefit of a contractual term in two cases:

1 If the contract expressly provides that they may do so.
2 If a term of the contract purports to confer a benefit, unless on a proper construction of the term it appears that it was not intended to be enforceable by the third party.

How could this affect the above situations?

■ It only applies to contracts made on or after 11 May 2000.

■ It will allow an action by a beneficiary where the contract or deed (the Act includes deeds – s. 7(3)), between the settlor and the trustee expressly conferred a benefit on the beneficiary.

This means that provided there was a contract and not just a promise a beneficiary may be able to enforce the obligation to constitute a trust in their favour. So the answer to Example 6.6 may be different and in Example 6.7 the volunteer might be able to sue under this Act as well as at common law, although there is doubt as to whether specific performance can be obtained under the Act.

■ Trustees' position where trust is incompletely constituted

What of Robert, the trustee in the above examples? Assuming that Miranda is unable to take action herself, can he do so on her behalf? The answer is probably no, although the cases do not give a definite answer: see, for example, *Re Pryce* [1917]; *Re Kay* [1939]; *Re Cook's Settlement Trusts* [1965].

Indirect constitution of a trust

KEY CASE

Re Ralli's Will Trust [1964] Ch 288 (HC)

Concerning: indirect constitution of a trust

Facts

(Simplified) The Trustee was also the executor under the will of the settlor/testator and the trust was held to be constituted.

Legal principle

A trust can be constituted if the trust property reaches the intended trustee in an indirect way (i.e. as in the above case where the trustee was also the executor) and one which was not intended by the settlor.

EXAM TIP

If the scenario has the same person as both the trustee under an unconstituted trust and as the executor under the settlor's will then look carefully to see if *Re Ralli* applies. This makes it easy to spot in an exam.

Three ways in which equity may assist a volunteer

EXAM TIP

These are exceptions to the principle that 'equity will not assist a volunteer'. Note that they deal with gifts but they can also be relevant to attempts to constitute a trust.

1 Rule in *Strong* v *Bird*

KEY CASE

Strong v *Bird* (1874) LR 18 Eq 315 (CA)

Concerning: perfecting an incomplete gift (i.e. one which has been promised but not made)

Facts

X had borrowed £1100 from his stepmother but did not repay £900 of it. Her will appointed him as her executor. ▶

Legal principle

Where there is an intention to make an immediate gift, or to release a debt, and that intention continues until the death then the appointment of the donee as executor perfects the gift/releases the debt. Therefore the debt of £900 owed by X to his stepmother was released.

Example 6.9

Pam promises Teresa that she will give Teresa her car. Pam then appoints Teresa her executor. On Pam's death Teresa can claim the car.

Suppose that before her death Pam had told her daughter, Sophie, that she could borrow the car. Here the rule in *Strong* v *Bird* would not apply as there needs to be a continuing intention to make an immediate gift (*Re Gonin* (1979)) and clearly this cannot now be the case.

Does this rule also apply to **administrators** appointed under intestacy? See *Re Gonin* (1979) (a very useful case for exams).

2 Donatio mortis causa (DMC)

This exception applies where a gift is made:

- in contemplation of death
- where the subject matter of the gift, or the means of control of it, or some essential indication of title, was delivered to the donee
- where there was an intention to make the gift conditional on death.

This topic is generally easy enough provided that you learn the above rules and the relevant case law.

One particularly important case is as follows:

KEY CASE

Sen v *Hedley* [1991] Ch 425 (CA)

Concerning: whether land can be the subject of a DMC

Facts

The deceased was terminally ill and said to the claimant (a very close friend for many years): 'The house is yours, Margaret. You have the keys. They are in your bag. The deeds are in a steel box.'

Legal principle

There can be a valid DMC of land and there was a valid DMC here as all the requirements were satisfied.

REVISION NOTE

The effect of a DMC is that pending the death of the donor the property is held on a constructive trust for the donee (see *Sen* v *Hedley*). Check Chapter 9 and make sure that you are clear what a constructive trust is.

3 Estoppel

Estoppel is a principle which also appears in land law but it may arise here in the context of incomplete gifts, e.g. where a promise to put land in another's name is not put in the required formality – see *Dillwyn v Llewellyn* (1862). Estoppel is considered in more detail in Chapter 9.

◼ **Chapter summary**: putting it all together

Test yourself

- ☐ Can you tick all the points from the **revision checklist** at the beginning of this chapter?
- ☐ Attempt the **sample question** from the beginning of this chapter using the answer guidelines below.
- ☐ Go to the **companion website** to access more revision support online, including interactive quizzes, sample questions with answer guidelines, 'you be the marker' exercises, flashcards and podcasts you can download.

Answer guidelines

See the problem question at the start of the chapter.

Approaching the question

Valid transfers by John? Check formalities. If not, DMC? Estoppel? Note Fiona is executor.

Important points to include

- Belinda: No valid transfer. Here involved and LPA 1925, s. 52(1) must be complied with – deed required and no deed. Could be a DMC – note *Sen* v *Hedley* can have a DMC of land – but it appears to be an outright gift and not one conditional on death. Therefore it fails and the property remains in Joshua's estate.

- Charles: Is this a declaration that Joshua now holds on trust for Charles? Older cases may be against this (e.g. see *Richards* v *Delbridge*) but note the more relaxed view taken in *Choithram*. If it is not a valid declaration of trust then the property forms part of Joshua's estate.

- Fiona: Possibility of a DMC but there is no delivery of any indication of title. Could be estoppel: set out the requirements for a valid estoppel but do not come to a definite conclusion – evidence not enough to decide.

- Laura: Could be a DMC but again looks like an outright gift. Apply *Pennington* v *Waine* and *Re Rose* and see if could be valid on the principle that Joshua has done all that he can to transfer title to the property.

- If Fiona is appointed executrix then the gift to her is perfected – *Strong* v *Bird*.

- If Joshua died six months later when playing tennis then he must have recovered from his original illness and so, if there were any valid DMCs they would have been revoked.

 Make your answer stand out

This answer used the recent cases of *Choithram* and *Pennington* but you will gain extra marks if you can show how the approach in earlier cases differed. In addition, the judges in the Court of Appeal in *Pennington* gave different reasons for their decisions; look at these and discuss them.

READ TO IMPRESS

Clarke, P. (2001) All ER Review 265.

Clarke, P. (2002) All ER Review 229.

Gardner, S. (2006) 'The Remedial Discretion in Proprietary Estoppel – Again', 122 LQR 492.

Garton, J. (2003) 'The role of the trust mechanism in the Rule in Re Rose', 87 Conv. 364.

Halliwell, M. (2003) 'Perfecting imperfect gifts and trusts: have we reached the end of the Chancellor's foot?', 87 Conv. 192.

Hopkins, J. (2001) 'Constitution of Trusts – A Novel Point', 60 CLJ 483.

NOTES

6 CONSTITUTION

NOTES

Secret and half-secret trusts

7

Revision checklist

Essential points you should know:

- [ ] the distinction between secret and half-secret trusts
- [ ] why equity enforces secret and half-secret trusts
- [ ] the requirements for the validity of secret and half-secret trusts
- [ ] the importance of knowing whether these trusts are express or constructive
- [ ] the rules on what happens to the property when either of these trusts fail

■ Topic map

Introduction

There is often a problem question on these trusts.

In addition, this topic is an excellent illustration of a familiar maxim of equity: *equity will not allow a statute to be used as an engine of fraud* and so it is useful for essay questions.

Secret trusts form one of the four interlocking topics in trusts law and you should be prepared for a question to involve one or more of these topics. A reminder of what they are:

- three certainties
- formalities
- secret trusts
- constitution.

A question on secret trusts will not be likely to involve constitution but it could well involve the others. If so, the secret trusts issue will be the main one but you will be expected to deal with the others as well.

ASSESSMENT ADVICE

Essay questions   An essay question on secret and half-secret trusts could involve either:

1 a question on the theoretical basis of these trusts, or
2 a question based on one of the maxims: equity will not allow a statute to be used as an instrument of fraud (the statute here is the Wills Act 1837) or equity looks to the intent rather than the form, i.e. equity looks at the intention to create a trust rather than whether the formalities have been complied with – here those in the Wills Act 1837.

The moral is to think clearly about just why these trusts should be enforced and be able to weigh up the opposing arguments.

Problem questions   Problems will require you to say if the trust is valid and so you must be able to apply the tests for the validity of a secret and half-secret trust. Almost certainly the problem will involve one or both of the decisions in *Re Keen* [1937] and *Re Stead* [1900] and, if you decide that the trust is valid, there will be subsidiary points to watch for: for example, did trustees/beneficiaries witness the will? Is it a trust of land? You will also need to bear in mind the requirements of certainty, as explained above.

■ Sample question

Can you answer this question? Below is a typical problem question that could arise on this topic. Guidelines on answering the question are included at the end of the chapter while a sample essay question and guidance on tackling it can be found on the companion website.

PROBLEM QUESTION

Jennifer is aged 87 and had been told by her doctor that she may not have long to live. She has substantial savings, together with her house, 'The Laurels', which she does not wish to leave to any of her family, whom she dislikes, and so she explains the problem to her friends Mabel and Fanny. She tells them both that she intends to make them beneficiaries under her will but that she will let them know what to do with their bequests later. They are both puzzled but agree to help if they can. Jennifer telephones Mabel later that day and they have a long conversation.

Jennifer executes her will on 1 February, three days after she had spoken to Mabel and Fanny. In it, she leaves £50,000 and 'The Laurels' to Mabel to be used for 'the purposes which we have discussed' and £100,000 to Fanny. Mabel and Fanny were witnesses to the will. The local hospital is named as the residuary beneficiary.

Later that day, Jennifer gave Mabel an envelope with the words written on it: 'This contains important instructions. Open immediately on my death but not before.'

On 3 February Jennifer wrote to Fanny and told her that of the £100,000, £90,000 should be held on trust for all the employees and their relatives of Barset College to be distributed among them at Fanny's discretion. The other £10,000 is a gift to Fanny in memory of the good times that she and Jennifer shared together. Fanny received this letter on 4 February.

Jennifer died on 5 February. Mabel found that 'The Laurels' is to be held on trust for Alf, Jennifer's son, and the £50,000 is to be held on trust for Jack, an old friend of Jennifer. However, Jack predeceased Jennifer.

Advise Mabel and Fanny on whether the trusts are valid and, if not, for whose benefit the property should be held.

■ The distinction between secret and half-secret trusts

Example 7.1

John wishes to leave £10,000 to his girlfriend Fifi but does not want his wife to know of this, as she is unaware of his relationship with Fifi. Accordingly, he decides to leave the property to someone who will hold it on trust to carry out his wishes.

John's will reads: 'I leave £10,000 to Steve'.

This is a **secret trust** as the will does not disclose either the existence or the details of the trust. Ask the question: on reading the will, would anyone know that there was a trust? If not, the trust is secret.

Example 7.2

Susan wishes to make a will as she is going into hospital for a major operation but she cannot decide who to leave her property to.

Susan's will reads: 'I leave all my property to Deborah on the trusts which I have declared to her.'

This is a **half-secret trust** as, although the will discloses the existence of a trust it does not disclose the details of it.

EXAM TIP

If you are faced with a problem question on secret trusts in the exam, first look at the words of the will, as these will tell you if the trust is secret or half-secret. The rules for them are different in some respects and so it is vital to be clear at the outset which category the trust falls into.

EXAM TIP

The words used by the settlor should be looked at carefully to see that certainty of intention to create a trust is disclosed (e.g. in the will). If there is, then the trust will be half-secret.

If you are in doubt whether the words disclose a secret or a half-secret trust you should answer for both although it may be that the court would decide that there was enough evidence of an obligation for there to be a half-secret trust. In *Blackwell* v *Blackwell* [1929] the will used the word 'purposes'.

■ Rationale for secret and half-secret trusts

The fraud rationale

This is that secret trusts must be enforced by equity to prevent fraud.

 Make your answer stand out

Look at the judgment of Lord Westbury in *McCormick* v *Grogan* (1869) for a clear statement of the fraud rationale.

EXAM TIP

Secret trusts are excellent examples of the maxim 'equity will not allow a statute to be used as an engine of fraud' and an essay question may ask you to discuss this maxim. Make a list of examples of this maxim, and others that you come across, to be cited in answers. See Chapters 5 and 9 for further examples.

The intention rationale

This is that equity enforces half-secret trusts to give effect to the intentions of the settlor.

 Make your answer stand out

See the judgment of Lord Buckmaster in *Blackwell* v *Blackwell* [1929] for a clear statement of the intention rationale.

EXAM TIP

Secret trusts normally arise in the context of gifts by will and these form the main part of this chapter. They can also arise when an *inter vivos* gift is made. An exam question will almost certainly involve gifts by will but an answer to an essay question will be improved by a discussion of secret trusts arising *inter vivos*.

Requirements for the validity of a secret trust

The requirements are as follows:

- the **intention** of the testator to create a trust (together with the trust property being certain and the objects of the trust satisfying the test for certainty of objects)
- **communication** of that intention to the intended trustees in the lifetime of the testator
- **acceptance** of the trust by the intended trustees either expressly or by acquiescence.

See *Ottaway* v *Norman* [1972] where these were clearly stated.

Intention, subject matter and objects

We saw above that certainty of intention is relevant in deciding whether the trust was secret or half-secret. In addition, all the three certainties must be present for both secret and half-secret trusts. It is possible, however, that there may be a doubt over this.

Suppose that Susan's will said: 'I leave all my property to Deborah for the purposes which I have indicated to her.' This may look like a secret trust at first sight but the words 'purposes which I have indicated to her' do not clearly disclose the existence of a trust. Your knowledge of the rules on certainty of intention will be needed here.

Look at the words used in *Gold* v *Hill* (1998) where there was sufficient intention.

Communication

EXAM TIP

Always check that you have found a home for the property! If there is no valid trust decide where it will go. Where the secret trust was not communicated then it will be a gift to the intended trustee (donee).

Wallgrave v *Tebbs* (1855) 2 K & J 313 (HC)

Concerning: communication of secret trusts

Facts

The facts of this case do not aid an understanding of the legal principle.

Legal principle

In cases of secret trusts the trust must be communicated during the lifetime of the testator so here the intended trustee took the property absolutely, as there was no trust.

Communication will be valid where the testator delivers a sealed envelope to the intended trustee with the direction: 'Not to be opened until after my death.' (*Re Keen* [1937].) However, the intended trustee must know that the envelope contains details of the trust and it must be handed to her during the lifetime of the testator.

A halfway situation

The testator tells the intended trustee that she is to hold the property on trust but does not communicate the details of the trust. Here the intended trustee cannot take the property beneficially, as she knows that she is a trustee and so she holds it on a resulting trust for the testator's estate (*Re Boyes* [1884]).

Acceptance

The intended trustee must accept the trust either expressly or by acquiescence and so silence will be enough for acceptance – contrast the position in contract. In *Moss* v *Cooper* (1861) Wood VC referred to: 'Acquiescence either by words of consent or silence.'

■ Requirements for the validity of a half-secret trust

The only difference between the requirements for the validity of a half-secret trust and a secret trust is the rules on communication. Thus you already know two of the three requirements.

In the case of half-secret trusts intention to create a trust will appear in the will itself.

Communication in half-secret trusts

This is a favourite area for exam questions because the law is uncertain. There are two possible rules:

■ Rule one (which is probably the law): Communication must be before the date of the execution of the will (*Re Keen*).

If this is the rule then the difference between the two types of trusts can be seen in Figure 7.1.

Figure 7.1

| Date of will | | Date of death | |

Both types can be communicated   Only secret trust can be communicated   Neither can be communicated

■ Rule two: If the will states a time of communication then the trust must be communicated at that time. This rule also arises from *Re Keen* and the fact that there are two rules arises from the judgment of Lord Wright in *Re Keen*.

Re Keen [1937] Ch 236 (CA)

Concerning: communication of a half-secret trust

Facts

The testator left £10,000 to trustees to hold on trust and to be disposed of by them among such persons, etc. as may 'be notified by me to them during my lifetime'.

Legal principle

■ The words 'to be notified by me' indicated an intention to make future communications and this was invalid as communication must be before the will.
■ The actual communication was before the will and this conflicted with the words to 'be notified'.

A final point is that where a codicil is later added to a will this 'republishes the will' so that the date of the will is now the date of the codicil. This can affect the rules on communication:

Example 7.3

Date of will: 1 January

Date of communication: 1 February

Communication is too late if Rule one is applied.

Date of Codicil: 1 March

Therefore:

Date of will now 1 March

Therefore communication valid

Where the half-secret trust is not validly communicated the property is held on a resulting trust for the beneficiaries (e.g. the hospital in the exam question).

Position where the trust is communicated to only one of two or more trustees

Re Stead [1900] 1 Ch 237 (HC)

Concerning: communication of a secret trust to some but not all intended trustees

Facts

The facts of this case do not aid an understanding of the legal principle.

Legal principle

■ Where communication is to one of two joint tenants and this takes place *before* the will then all joint tenants are bound
■ Where communication is to one of two joint tenants *after* the will then only the one to whom the trust is communicated is bound
■ Where communication is to one of two tenants in common then only the one to whom the trust is communicated is bound.

Example 7.4

Jason leaves £10,000 to Mark and Anthony. Before Jason executed the will he told Mark, but not Anthony, that he wanted the £10,000 to be held for the benefit of his daughter, Mary.

Mark and Anthony are joint tenants, as there are no words of severance, and so they are both bound. If the gift had been to Mark and Anthony in equal shares then they would have been tenants in common and so only Mark would have been bound. He would hold £5,000 on trust for Mary and Anthony would take the other £5,000 beneficially.

EXAM TIP

It is unlikely that the distinction between tenants in common and joint tenants will involve you learning fine points of distinction between them. Look for words of severance: if they are there the gift is to tenants in common, if they are not there the gift is to joint tenants.

Make your answer stand out

Refer to the criticism of this rule by Perrins (1972).

EXAM TIP

For extra marks learn why this rule is felt to be unsatisfactory and what might replace it.

▉ Other rules

These are as follows:

■ Where there is an addition to the trust this must be communicated, e.g. if an additional sum is to be held on trust (*Re Colin Cooper* [1939])

■ Where a beneficiary under a secret trust witnesses the will this does not affect the gift as the trust is outside (*dehors*) the will (*Re Young* [1951])

■ Where a person is named as trustee in a half-secret trust and also witnesses it this will not affect the trust as they are not named as a beneficiary but a trustee

■ Where a person is a trustee under a secret trust and witnesses the will then they cannot take the property as they appear in the will to be beneficiaries

■ Where a beneficiary under a secret or half-secret trust dies before the testator the gift does not lapse but passes to their estate (*Re Gardner* [1920]). Had the gift been in a will then in most cases the gift would have lapsed

■ There is doubt as to whether a person can bring evidence to show that they were intended to benefit under a secret or half-secret trust. In *Re Rees* [1950] it was held that this was not possible but in *Re Tyler's Fund Trusts* [1967] it was suggested that such evidence is admissible

■ The death of the secret trustee before the death of the testator causes the trust to fail as the gift to the trustee lapses. But if the trust is half-secret then the trust can be valid as the will itself indicates a trust.

! **Don't be tempted to...**

Be sure to mention that the decision in *Re Gardner* is often felt to be wrong as at the date of the beneficiary's death the trust was not constituted. This can only happen on the beneficiary's death.

■ Are secret and half-secret trusts express or constructive?

This point is important if the trust concerns land, as in an exam question. The rule is probably that a secret trust is constructive as it is imposed to prevent fraud. A half-secret trust is probably express as it is declared on the will.

This means that secret trusts of land need not be in writing as constructive trusts of land need not be (s. 53(2), LPA 1925), but half-secret trusts as express trusts are governed by s. 53(1)(b), LPA 1925 which requires trusts of land other than resulting and constructive trusts to be evidenced by writing.

REVISION NOTE

Go back to Chapter 5 and check that you are clear on the formalities rules.

■ Chapter summary: putting it all together

Test yourself

- ☐ Can you tick all the points from the **revision checklist** at the beginning of this chapter?
- ☐ Attempt the **sample question** from the beginning of this chapter using the answer guidelines below.
- ☐ Go to the **companion website** to access more revision support online, including interactive quizzes, sample questions with answer guidelines, 'you be the marker' exercises, flashcards and podcasts you can download.

Answer guidelines

See the problem question at the start of the chapter.

Approaching the question

Problem questions in this area usually contain a number of different issues and so there is plenty of opportunity to gain a really good mark. However, it is essential to have a very clear and logical structure to your answer otherwise you could get your points in the wrong order with disastrous effects on your marks! Make a plan of your answer and stick to it!

Important points to include

Trust to Mabel

Take the words 'for the purposes of'. Do they indicate a trust or not? An average answer will say that they do, which is probably the case, and this will mean that:

- There is definitely intention to create a trust.
- This is definitely a half-secret trust.

An excellent answer will explain that the words 'on trust' are not used and so there is the possibility that:

- There is no intention, unless the conversation in the opening paragraph indicates sufficient intention.
- Even if there is intention, which is probably the case, the trust may be secret.

If there is some doubt, then proceed for both types:

- On the basis that the trust is half-secret, there is intention, as indicated in the will but communication is doubtful. The will states that the gift to Mabel is to be 'used for the purposes which we have discussed' which indicates a past communication. In fact, communication to Mabel is by an envelope which is not to be opened until Jennifer's death and the envelope is given to Mabel on the same day as the will was executed but later on.

- Under Rule one communication appears to be too late but, as we saw above, *Re Keen* also established that communication could be a sealed envelope not to be opened until the testator's death provided that the testator knows that the envelope contains the details of the trust. Here the words 'important instructions' could be taken as indicating that the envelope does contain details of a trust but it is not definite. The fact that communication is later in the day can probably be overlooked but the point is not decided.

- Under Rule two communication is probably invalid as the will says 'the purposes which we have discussed' unless the initial discussion in the first paragraph can be taken as communication, which must be doubtful.

- There is probably valid communication on the basis of *Re Keen* but an excellent answer would also point out that if Rule two applies then communication is not valid as the time of communication conflicts with the will. However, there is also the long telephone conversation between Jennifer and Mabel: an excellent answer would point out that this may have contained communication.

- On the basis that the trust is secret there is valid communication as the handing over of the envelope amounts to communication before the death of the testator.

- If there is no valid communication, then Mabel will take on a resulting trust for the estate (the residuary beneficiary – the hospital). If it is valid then on we go.

- Is there a valid acceptance? There is no express acceptance but it can be implied (*Moss* v *Cooper* (1861)) and after the initial conversation the long telephone conversation might have contained an acceptance.

- As the trust concerns land, if it is half-secret then it is express and under s. 53(1)(b), LPA 1925 the trust of 'The Laurels' must be in writing. The bare details are in the will, which is, of course, written and, if this is sufficient, then the requirements are satisfied. An excellent answer would point out that a failure to comply with s. 53(1)(b) renders the trust unenforceable and not void.

- If the trust is valid, the death of Jack will not cause the trust to fail and the gift to him will go to his estate (*Re Gardner*). (A good answer might point out that this case is considered doubtful.)

Trust to Fanny

This is secret and appears valid: communication is before Jennifer's death, intention appears from the will (use of word 'trust' and acceptance can be implied).

Two problems arise:

1 Does the gift to employees, etc. satisfy the test of certainty of objects (*McPhail* v *Doulton* [1971] – see Chapter 3)? If not, a resulting trust for the estate – in this case the hospital.
2 Can Fanny adduce evidence that she was intended to be a beneficiary? Consider *Re Rees* and *Re Tyler's Fund Trusts*.

▶

Make your answer stand out

Pay very close attention to the actual words used in the trust. See the discussion above on whether there is any possibility that the trust to Mabel could be a secret trust.

READ TO IMPRESS

Critchley, P. (1999) 'Instruments of Fraud: Testamentary Dispositions and Secret Trusts', 115 LQR 631. A useful look at the whole area.

Meager, R. 'Secret trusts: Do they have a Future?', 87 Conv. 203. Interesting research showing that secret trusts are important in practice.

Perrins, B. (1972) 'Can You Keep Half a Secret?', 88 LQR 225. Demonstrates that the principles in *Re Stead* rest on a tenuous historical basis.

NOTES

Resulting trusts

Revision checklist

Essential points you should know:

- [ ] the distinction between express trusts and resulting/constructive trusts
- [ ] the theories that explain the basis of resulting trusts
- [ ] when a resulting trust arises where property is put into the name of another and why this is so
- [ ] when a presumption of advancement arises and the significance of these today
- [ ] when a resulting trust can arise where the beneficial interest is not disposed of
- [ ] the importance of the *Quistclose* case

Topic map

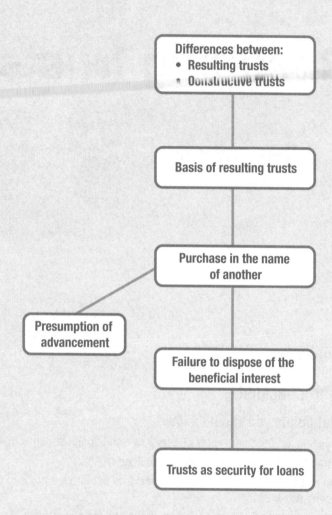

Differences between:
• Resulting trusts
• Constructive trusts

Basis of resulting trusts

Purchase in the name
of another

Presumption of
advancement

Failure to dispose of the
beneficial interest

Trusts as security for loans

A printable version of this topic map is available from www.pearsoned.co.uk/lawexpress

■Introduction

This chapter and the next one, on constructive trusts, should be considered together.

This is because:

■ There is a clear dividing line between express trusts, on the one hand, and resulting and constructive trusts on the other (see below). You may get a question on this point.

■ In some cases, and especially those involving trusts of the home, there can be uncertainty whether the trust should be classified as resulting or constructive. Trusts of the home are dealt with in Chapter 9.

ASSESSMENT ADVICE

Essay questions This is a likely area for essays which could be on:

■ The basis of resulting trusts. This area is dealt with below and you should ensure that you understand the various theories, making sure that you can explain the basic idea behind them. You should then move on to relating the theories to the cases.

■ The basis of *Quistclose* trusts.

■ Both resulting and constructive trusts looking at their common features and how they differ.

Problem questions A problem question could link with material on constructive trusts, an obvious area being trusts of the home, or deal with *Quistclose* trusts.

■Sample question

Could you answer this question? Below is a typical essay question that could arise on this topic. Guidelines on answering the question are included at the end of the chapter, whilst a sample problem question and guidance on tackling it can be found on the companion website.

'Resulting trusts are a rag-bag of different situations with no clear principle to explain them.'

Do you agree?

Differences between express trusts and resulting and constructive trusts

The common feature of both resulting and constructive trusts is that, unlike express trusts, they are not created by the express agreement of the parties as evidenced in a trust deed, or some other writing, or, except in the case of trusts of land or an interest in land (s. 53(1)(b), LPA 1925), orally. One possible exception is a secret trust (see Chapter 7) which is generally considered to be constructive but does arise from agreement.

REVISION NOTE

Go back to Chapter 7 and make sure that you are clear about what a secret trust is.

Moffat (2009: 606) sets out these distinctions between express trusts on the one hand, and resulting and constructive trusts on the other:

- Functional. Express trusts are often employed as a planning device but imputed trusts are ways of resolving disputes over ownership or entitlement to property.

- Formal. Express trusts must comply with certain formalities such as s. 53(1)(c), LPA 1925. Imputed trusts are not affected by these (s. 53(2), LPA 1925).

We could also point to a substantive distinction. Express trusts arise because of some expression of intention by a property owner but imputed trusts arise by operation of some legal rule. However, this particular distinction breaks down in cases of disputes over the family home where intention plays a significant role.

REVISION NOTE

Go back to Chapter 5 and check that you know and understand what s. 53(1)(b), s. 53(1)(c) and s. 53(2), LPA 1925 say.

The above points could form an excellent framework for an answer to an exam question that asks you to discuss the differences between express trusts on the one hand, and resulting and constructive trusts on the other.

Resulting trusts

Basis of resulting trusts

KEY DEFINITION: Resulting trust

The beneficial interest results to, or jumps back to, the settlor who created the trust. The basis of an action founded on a resulting trust is therefore that one is seeking to recover one's own property.

The idea behind **resulting trusts** is strange: a person (X) gives property to another (Y) and then Y ends up holding it on trust for X.

Theories to explain the basis of resulting trusts

1 Megarry J in *Re Vandervell's Trusts (No. 2)* [1974]: two types of resulting trust:

Automatic	Presumed
Nothing to do with the intentions of the settlor (e.g. where no certainty of objects) – see Chapter 3.	Where property transferred to another for no consideration (i.e. nothing given or promised in return) but no words of gift used. Megarry J felt that these did arise from the presumed intention of the settlor. This chapter contains examples of these.

Chambers (1997) points out, however, that resulting trusts are concerned with the intention of the settlor as one reason why they arise is that the settlor does not intend the property to go to the trustee (1997: 47). There is a more fundamental objection pointed out by Swadling (2008): nothing is automatic in the law. The trust does not arise automatically but because the courts say that it does.

2 Lord Browne-Wilkinson in *Westdeutsche Landesbank Girozentrale* v *Islington LBC* [1996]: resulting trusts arise from the common intention of the parties.

EXAM TIP

Joan transfers £100 to Penny to hold on trust but fails to specify the trusts. The £100 is held on trust by Penny for Joan.

 Make your answer stand out

Swadling (2008) points out that intention only arises in a negative sense as the initial intention, in the above example, was for Penny to hold the £100 on trust and so there is only a presumed intention of a resulting trust as the first intention could not be carried out. In addition can we just assume that this was the intention?

In *Re Vinogradoff* [1935] the testatrix had transferred an £800 War Loan which was in her own name into the joint names of herself and her four-year-old daughter. After the testatrix died it was held that even though the daughter had not been appointed a trustee she still held it on a resulting trust for the testatrix's estate. The fundamental point is that the court did not say that it came to this decision because of the testatrix's intentions.

3 Chambers (1997): all resulting trusts should be considered as arising from the presumption of *the lack of any intention* by the transferor to pass any beneficial interest to the transferee when the transferee has not provided the entire consideration for the property. Thus in the example above the resulting trust operates because Joan did not intend to benefit Penny.

4 Swadling (2008): Chambers' view is wrong. His argument is that the word 'presumption' needs clarification. He argues that a true presumption arises where proof of one fact generates proof of another fact without the need for further evidence. In the case of resulting trusts where the transferor puts property into the name of another the evidence is that equity originally rested the presumption on evidence that the transferor declared a trust in his own favour. 'Automatic' resulting trusts, according to Swadling, seem to have no clear foundation. It is usually considered that, on any transfer, only the *legal interest* passes to the transferee. Where the resulting trust arises from that transfer, then a new equitable interest arises and this is held for the transferor (see Chambers (above)). Look at the *Quistclose* case (below) to test this idea.

 Don't be tempted to...

Don't forget to consider what happens to the beneficial interest.

■ Cases where a resulting trust can arise

Purchase in the name of another

The basic equitable rule is that where property is purchased in the name of another then there is a presumption that the other person holds it on a resulting trust for the purchaser.

> **Example 8.1**
>
> X buys a house and puts it in Y's name. There is a presumption that Y holds it on trust for X. This can be rebutted by proof that a gift was intended. (See *Dyer* v *Dyer* (1788).)

Hodgson v *Marks* (1971) is a good example of this point where the owner transferred her house into the name of her lodger and it was held that there was a resulting trust in her favour. Note the remarks of Russell LJ on the relationship between undue influence and resulting trusts.

Trusts of the home may come into this category. See Chapter 9 for the views of Lord Neuberger in *Stack* v *Dowden* and the decision in *Laskar* v *Laskar* on the applicability of resulting trusts to deciding the beneficial interests in the home.

Presumption of advancement

The idea is that, in contrast to the example above where there is a presumption of a resulting trust, here there is a presumption that the person making the transfer intends an outright gift (an advancement).

The situations where a presumption can arise were rather old fashioned (e.g. they applied where a husband transfers property to his wife but not vice versa and to advancements by a father (but not a mother) to their children). However, in *Pecore* v *Pecore* (2007) the Canadian Supreme Court held that they could also apply to an advancement by a mother. The cases also held that the presumption ceases when the child becomes an independent adult.

Read Andrews (2007) on the possiblility that the presumption contravenes Art. 5, Protocol 7 of the European Convention on Human Rights (equality of rights and responsibilities of spouses). The extra dimension which this kind of thinking brings to an answer can really boost your marks.

An interesting area is where the presumption of a resulting trust appears to collide with the maxim that equity does not assist a person with unclean hands.

KEY CASE

Tinsley v *Milligan* [1994] 1 AC 340 (HL)

Concerning: transfers of property for unlawful purposes

Facts

A house was bought with money provided by two women (X and Y) but was only put into the name of X so that Y could (fraudulently) claim housing benefit. Y claimed that the property was held for her on a resulting trust by virtue of her contributions.

Legal principle

The issue was the conduct which Y had to rely on to support her claim of a resulting trust. If it was her fraud then she could not claim a resulting trust, in view of the principle stated above. However, here she only had to rely on her contributions to the purchase price and so her claim succeeded as her fraud was, as a matter of evidence, irrelevant.

 Make your answer stand out

This decision of the House of Lords has been strongly criticised. Look, for example, at Buckley (1994) but also note a contrary view expressed by Enonchong (1995). You should also look at the judgments of the Court of Appeal, which differed from those of the majority of the House of Lords: see *Tinsley* v *Milligan* [1992] Ch 310 CA.

 Make your answer stand out

Consultation Paper 154 published by the Law Commission in 1999: *Illegal Transactions: The Effect of Illegality on Contracts and Trusts*, recommends that the courts should be given discretion in these cases but also sets five criteria at paragraph 1.19. Look at these carefully!

Note also *Tinker* v *Tinker* [1970].

Failure to dispose of the beneficial interest

Example 8.3

Re Osaba (1979): a trust was set up to maintain two women and to educate a third. After the death of the first two and the completion of the education of the third the surplus went absolutely to the third. Yet in *Re Abbott* (1982) a fund to maintain two ladies which had a surplus went to the subscribers to it. Note also *Re Gillingham Bus Disaster Fund* [1959] in Chapter 10.

REVISION NOTE

Look at Chapter 10 where this issue is looked at in connection with failure of charitable trusts. Compare the rules when a charitable fund fails with when a non-charitable fund fails.

Trusts as security for loans

KEY CASE

Barclays Bank Ltd v ***Quistclose Investments Ltd*** [1970] AC 567 (HL)

Concerning: when a loan can be held on a resulting trust for the lender

Facts

Quistclose lent money to a company (Rolls Razor) for the sole purpose of enabling it to pay dividends and this money was held in a separate bank account. The company went into liquidation before the dividend was paid.

Legal principle

Where a loan is made for a specific purpose which fails then a resulting trust may arise for the lender, in this case Quistclose. The effect is to give the lender priority over the borrower's creditors if, as here, the borrower goes into liquidation.

KEY CASE

Re Farepak Food and Gifts Ltd (in administration) (2006) EWHC 3272 (HC)

Concerning: possible application of the Quistclose principle

Facts

Under a Christmas hamper scheme operated by Farepak, throughout 2006 customers placed orders for hampers with Farepak's agents who then passed them on to Farepak. On 11 October 2006 Farepak decided to cease trading. Before it went into administration the directors attempted to 'ring fence' money which was received by Farepak so that it could be returned to customers. They did this by a declaration of trust but did it actually create a trust?

Legal principle

The *Quistclose* principle could not apply because the money had been received by the Farepak agents (not Farepak) and when it was received there was no suggestion that it was to be kept separate from other money. Thus there could be no *Quistclose* trust as there was, in effect, no trust property. There could only have been such a trust had the money from customers been kept in a separate fund so that it could not be touched until the customers had received their hampers.

KEY CASE

Templeton Insurance Ltd. v *Penningtons* (2006) EWHC 685

Concerning: application of the Quistclose principle

Facts

An insurance company (X) deposited £500,000 with solicitors (Y) 'for the express purpose of completion' of a property to be acquired by a client. Y used some of the money for other purposes as the actual price was only around £236,000.

Legal principle

Y were held liable to return to X that part of the £500,000 not used for the purchase as it was held for X on a resulting trust under the Quistclose principle.

✓ Make your answer stand out

The principle in the *Quistclose* case is controversial. Why should the lender in *Quistclose* have priority? It may be mere chance that the loan is not spent as intended. If it is spent the lender loses priority. Look at other cases on the *Quistclose* principle (e.g. *Carreras Rothmans Ltd* v *Freeman Matthews Treasure Ltd* (1985)) and at Millett (1998). Another issue is who are the beneficiaries? Was it the shareholders in the *Quistclose* case?

REVISION NOTE

Check the beneficiary principle in Chapter 4.

The *Re Farepak* case is also relevant to express trusts (Chapter 3) and constructive trusts (Chapter 9). It could form an excellent illustration, in an essay question, of the modern application of the law of trusts.

■ **Chapter summary**: putting it all together

Test yourself

- ☐ Can you tick all the points from the **revision checklist** at the beginning of this chapter?
- ☐ Attempt the **sample question** from the beginning of this chapter using the answer guidelines below.
- ☐ Go to the **companion website** to access more revision support online, including interactive quizzes, sample questions with answer guidelines, 'you be the marker' exercises, flashcards and podcasts you can download.

Answer guidelines

See the essay question at the start of the chapter.

Approaching the question

This question requires you to know and understand the situations when a resulting trust arises and then to see if they can be linked by any coherent theory. As ever, you will not gain many marks if you just go through the situations and describe them. Instead, think about each type of trust and relate it to the theories explained at the start of this chapter.

Important points to include

For example, you could begin with the theory of Lord Browne Wilkinson that resulting trusts can be explained on the basis of the common intention of the parties. Take a case and see if you think that this is the basis. Use the same approach for the 'automatic' theory of Megarry J in *Re Vandervell's Trusts (No. 2)* [1974] and Chambers' theory that they arise from lack of intention. Do not mention too many cases – five or six overall thoroughly discussed and all making different points is better than twice as many dealt with superficially.

 Make your answer stand out

A really clear analysis of cases in relation to the different theories is what is required here.

READ TO IMPRESS

Andrews, G. (2007) 'The Presumption of Advancement: Equity, Equality and Human Rights', 71 Conv. 340.

Buckley, R. (1994) 'Social Security Fraud as Illegality', 110 LQR 3.

Chambers, R. (1997) *Resulting Trusts*, Oxford: Clarendon Press.

Enonchong, N. (1995) 'Title Claims and Illegal Transactions', 111 LQR 135.

Millett, P. (1998) 'Equity's place in the Law of Commerce', 114 LQR 214.

Moffat, G. (2009) *Trusts Law: Text and Materials*, 5th edn, Cambridge: Cambridge University Press.

Swadling, W. (2008) 'Explaining Resulting Trusts', 124 LQR 72.

NOTES

NOTES

Constructive trusts and estoppel

9

Revision checklist

Essential points you should know:

☐ the basis on which constructive trusts can arise

☐ how to identify and explain, with examples, the main situations where equity imposes a constructive trust: profits made by a fiduciary; where statute is used as an instrument of fraud; receipt of trust property by a third party

☐ how to identify other situations where a constructive trust has been imposed

☐ how to distinguish between a remedial and an institutional constructive trust

■ Topic map

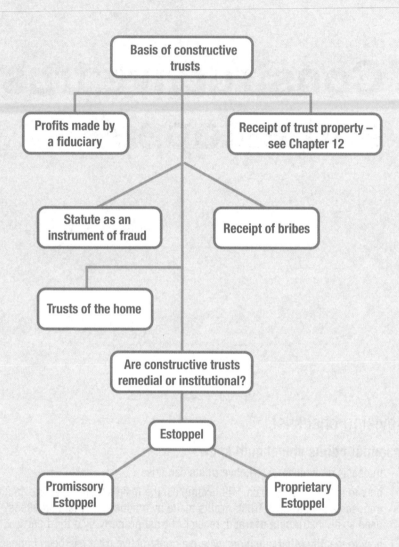

A printable version of this topic map is available from **www.pearsoned.co.uk/lawexpress**

■Introduction

It is impossible to avoid this area in an exam paper!

You may get a straight question on it, or you will find that constructive trusts come up in other areas such as trustees, breach of trust, trusts of the family home, the nature of equity and the concept of a trust. In addition the notion of a constructive trust appears in secret trusts (are these constructive?) and in the constitution of a trust. (Where there is a *donatio mortis causa* (DMC) then this can give rise to a constructive trust.) In short, if there is one area to revise carefully, this is it! In any answer you need to be aware that there is a continuing debate about the rationale of constructive trusts. Is their development tied to the fiduciary principle or is the trust a wide-ranging remedial weapon to be used where justice demands? Read this chapter with this point in mind.

ASSESSMENT ADVICE

Essay questions A very familiar essay question is to ask whether there is any form of words which can explain all the circumstances when a constructive trust can arise. The answer is probably no, but you need to be able to discuss the possibilities and back up your answer with examples from the cases. This is one area where a really good knowledge of the main cases, and of any others which appeal to you, will pay dividends rather than a superficial knowledge of many cases.

Another essay scenario is to ask you to consider the difference between the institutional and the remedial constructive trust. Some of the debates here are a bit old fashioned but still worth knowing. The case of *Binions* v *Evans* [1972] was once an absolute staple of exam questions.

Problem questions One obvious area for a problem question is the situation where trust property has been parted with in breach of trust and where there may also be someone who has assisted in the breach. A possibility is to include with this a situation based on a *Boardman* v *Phipps* scenario.

▌Sample question

Could you answer this question? Below is a typical problem question that could arise on this topic. Guidelines on answering the question are included at the end of the chapter, whilst a sample essay question and guidance on tackling it can be found on the companion website.

PROBLEM QUESTION

Osbert is a trustee of a family trust. The trust owns shares in the Midland Optical Illusion Co. Ltd and, at a shareholders' meeting, Osbert meets Albert, a director. Albert suggests that the company is a good investment and so Osbert buys sufficient shares to give him a controlling interest in the company. At a subsequent meeting Osbert is appointed a paid director of the company.

The company has become increasingly profitable and so all of the shares have grown in value.

Advise the beneficiaries on any claims which they may have against Osbert.

▌Constructive trusts

What are they?

KEY DEFINITION: Constructive trusts

Millett (1998) defined these as arising 'whenever the circumstances are such that it would be unconscionable for the owner of the legal title to assert his own beneficial interest and deny the beneficial interest of another'.

Can we go further than this?

Another quote is by Lord Scott in *Yeoman's Row Management Ltd.* v *Cobbe* (2008):

It is impossible to prescribe exhaustively the circumstances sufficient to create a constructive trust but it is possible to recognise particular factual circumstances that will do so and also to recognise other factual circumstances that will not.

Essays often ask you if there is any all-embracing principle to explain when constructive trusts are imposed. The answer is probably no but do not forget to include in your answer trusts of the home, which are dealt with later in this chapter.

All we can do here is indicate some circumstances when a constructive trust may be imposed:

Profits made by a fiduciary

! Don't be tempted to...

Be sure you have a good grasp of the definition of a 'fiduciary'. The concept of a fiduciary and a fiduciary relationship is at the very heart of equity but attempts to define what a fiduciary is have met with difficulty. The term certainly covers relationships *other than those* of trustee and beneficiary and fiduciaries can include company directors and solicitors. A good place to start is Moffat (2009: 833–845).

- 'The fiduciary relationship is a concept in search of a principle' (Mason, 'Themes and prospects', in *Essays in Equity*, Finn, P. (ed.) (1985))
- The fiduciary concept is like 'an accordion ... it may be expanded, or compressed, to maintain the integrity of relationships perceived to be of importance to contemporary society' (Tan, D. (1995) 69 ALJ 440).

An excellent quote on trustees as fiduciaries is as follows:

[A trustee] is not, unless expressly provided, entitled to make a profit; he is not allowed to put himself in a position where his interest and duty conflict.

Lord Herschell in *Bray* v *Ford* [1896]

However, this has been called 'rather a counsel of prudence than a rule of equity'.

✓ Make your answer stand out

In *Motivex Ltd* v *Bulfield* [1988] Vinelott J observed that: 'I do not think that it is strictly accurate to say that a director owes a fiduciary duty to the company not to put himself in a position where his duty to the company may conflict with his personal interest or with his duty to another.' Thus Lord Herschell's words should perhaps be rephrased to say that where there is a conflict between personal interests and duty as a trustee then the duty is not to take advantage of that conflict and to consider only the interests of the trust. See Koh (2003).

KEY CASE

Keech v *Sandford* (1726) Sel Cas Ch 61 Ct of Chan

Concerning: persons in a fiduciary position must not use that position to make an unauthorised benefit for themselves

Facts

A trustee of a lease of a market was granted a renewal of the lease in his own name because the landlord did not wish to renew it on trust as the beneficiary was a minor who could not be bound by the usual covenants.

Legal principle

X held the renewed lease on trust for the minor even though X had neither acted fraudulently nor deprived the trust of any benefit.

KEY CASE

Boardman v *Phipps* [1967] 2 AC 46 (HL)

Concerning: same issue as in Keech v Sandford (1726) (above) but applied in a modern context

Facts

The trust owned a substantial holding of shares in a company and the appellants were dissatisfied with its performance. They obtained information, through this connection with the trust, about the company's affairs and as a result they decided to obtain control of the company by purchasing the remainder of its shares. Having done this they reorganised it and made considerable profits for themselves. The trust could not have bought the shares without seeking the sanction of the court and it did not consider doing this.

Legal principle

The appellants were held liable to account to the trust for the profits made because they were constructive trustees as they had used the trust shareholding to acquire the necessary information about the company and in addition the respondent beneficiary had not been kept fully informed of the situation. However the appellants had acted in good faith throughout and so should be allowed 'liberal payment' for their skill in the negotiations which had resulted in the trust acquiring a considerable benefit.

Make your answer stand out

Consider the position where a fiduciary acts for two principals with potentially conflicting interests. In *Bristol and West Building Society* v *Mothew (1998)* Millet LJ emphasised the need for the informed consent of both to act. See Conaglen (2009).

KEY CASE

Queensland Mines Ltd v *Hudson* (1978) 18 ALR 1 (PC)

Concerning: application of the principle in Keech v Sandford (1726) and Boardman v Phipps [1967] to company directors

Facts

The defendant, the managing director of the claimant company, had obtained licences for the claimant to develop some mines. When the claimant found itself unable to do so the defendant, with the claimant's full knowledge, took the licences himself and developed them.

Legal principle

The defendant was not liable to account for profits made because he had not deprived the claimant of any opportunity and had kept the claimant fully informed. It is, however, difficult to reconcile this decision with *Boardman* v *Phipps* [1967] and *Regal (Hastings) Ltd* v *Gulliver* (1942).

Note that s. 175 of the Companies Act 2006 now provides that a director must avoid acting in situations where he has an interest which conflicts, or possibly may conflict, with the interests of the company. Section 175 (4)(b) provides that this duty is not infringed if the matter has been authorised by the directors. You should mention these provisions in a discussion of the above cases. Although this restates what was the law anyway you will add to your marks by mentioning it.

Receipt of bribes

***Attorney General for Hong Kong* v *Reid* [1994] AC 324 (HL)**

Concerning: receipt of bribes by a person in a fiduciary position

Facts

Reid, a Crown prosecutor, took bribes and then used them to buy land.

Legal principle

Where a person receive bribes in breach of their fiduciary duty then they become a constructive trustee of them and so here the bribes were the property of their employer in equity. Thus the employer was entitled to claim the profits from the bribes when they were invested.

 Make your answer stand out

Although this decision clearly has much to commend it on the level of ensuring that a person who takes bribes does not benefit by simply investing them, it also has the result that where a person has taken bribes and invested the proceeds the employer can claim these. Thus if the person is bankrupt, as here, the employer is in a better position than the unsecured creditors of that person.

Joint ventures

Where X and Y agree to acquire and develop land jointly and Y acquires it in his own name with the agreement of X but *then* seeks to retain the land for his own benefit, the court will regard him as holding the land on trust for the joint venturers i.e. both X and Y (*Pallant* v *Morgan* (1952)).

Statute as an instrument of fraud

See Rochefoucauld v *Boustead* [1897] in Chapter 5. However, the next case shows that equity does not always intervene to set aside a statutory requirement: there may be other more important values at stake.

Midland Bank Trust Co. Ltd v *Green* [1981] AC 513 (HL)

Concerning: whether a statutory requirement should be set aside as it is an instrument of fraud

Facts

An option granted by a father to his son to purchase a farm had not been registered as required by the Land Charges Act 1972 and the father, having changed his mind about the sale, then carried out a 'sham' sale to his wife so that his son's option was then defeated.

Legal principle

The son's claim failed, Lord Wilberforce observing that 'it is not fraud to rely on legal rights conferred by an Act of Parliament'.

Trusts of the home

This is an important area for exams and can also arise in a land law exam. The courts have used the concepts of both resulting and constructive trusts. Here is an example based on a typical exam question.

Example 9.1

Jane and her boyfriend Tom moved into a house which was in Jane's name as she was able to get a mortgage. However, it was always intended to be their joint home and Jane said to Tom: 'This will be our joint home for life. We will settle here.' Tom agreed and said that as this was the case, he would pay the deposit. The house needed a great deal of renovation and Tom spent all of his spare time working on the house.

Two years later Jane met Algy and told Tom: 'Algy is the man in my life now. You will have to move out.'

Does Tom have any rights in the house?

Tom may have three claims:

1 Based on a resulting trust as he had contributed to the purchase of the house which was in Jane's name.
2 Based on a constructive trust based not only on his contributions to the purchase but the work which he did on the house.
3 Based on estoppel which will be similar to the constructive trust claim but emphasises detrimental reliance, i.e. he relied on Jane's statement. See below for a discussion of estoppel.

REVISION NOTE

Check Chapter 8 for resulting trusts and below for estoppel.

How does the law deal with this situation?

This is an excellent study in the development of constructive trusts which could be used to illustrate an essay question. The most recent leading case is *Stack* v *Dowden* (2007) where the basis of the claim was said to be a constructive trust. Note this quote from Lady Hale in *Stack* v *Dowden*. The fundamental principle is 'the search is to ascertain the parties' shared intentions, actual, inferred or imputed, with respect to the property in the light of their whole course of conduct in relation to it'.

EXAM TIP

Compare this approach with Lord Bridge's speech in *Lloyds Bank plc* v *Rosset* [1991]. Look also at the approach of the Court of Appeal in the 1970s under the leadership of Denning MR based on the remedial constructive trust. *Eves* v *Eves* [1975] is a very good (and memorable) example of this. Is Lady Hale's approach in *Stack* v *Dowden* any different?

Note that in *Laskar* v *Laskar* (2008) Lord Neuberger, who had dissented from Lady Hale's reasoning in *Stack* v *Dowden*, held that a resulting trust was appropriate where property had been purchased as an investment and not as a home.

Tom, in the example above, would have a valid claim under any of the three approaches above but what if he had neither made any contribution nor had Jane said that the house was to be their joint home?

EXAM TIP

Law express: Land Law gives further details of this area but in any discussion you could mention cases such as *Burns* v *Burns* (1984). Look at the facts and decide whether the claimant would fare any better under the test in *Stack* v *Dowden* and, if not, how the law might change to deal with her type of claim.

Make your answer stand out

The Law Commission made proposals for change in this area 'Cohabitation: The Financial Consequences of Relationship Breakdown' (Law Com. Report 307). However, on 6 March 2008 the Government announced that it was delaying any implementation of the scheme until it had assessed research findings on the effect of the Family Law (Scotland) Act 2006 which has similar provisions. In fact the changes in the law made by *Stack* v *Dowden* may make the need for legislation less pressing.

Are constructive trusts institutional or remedial?

In a series of cases in the 1970s Denning MR sought to develop what he called 'a constructive trust of a new model' (*Eves* v *Eves* (1975)). The existence of a fiduciary relationship was not required to found such a trust: instead one would be imposed 'whenever justice and good conscience require it ... it is an equitable remedy by which the court can enable an aggrieved party to obtain restitution' (Denning MR in *Hussey* v *Palmer* (1972)). The main areas in which the new model constructive trust has been used are in disputes over the home (see above) and the enforceability of contractual licences as in *Binions* v *Evans* [1972].

There are two objections to the new model constructive trust:

1　To look at a constructive trust as a remedy and not as a substantive institution is wrong because, even though constructive trusts have always been remedies in one sense (see the cases above), they have also been substantive trusts because the property is trust property and therefore if the trustee becomes bankrupt the beneficiaries take priority over the trustee's creditors.
2　The idea of imposing a constructive trust whenever justice requires leads to uncertainty. Mahon J memorably observed in the New Zealand case of *Carly* v *Farrelly* (1975): 'No stable system of jurisprudence can permit a litigant's claim to justice to be consigned to the formless void of individual moral opinion.'

The new model constructive trust was firmly rejected by the Court of Appeal in *Halifax Building Society* v *Thomas* (1995) and *Re Polly Peck International plc (No. 2)* (1998) and you should also note *Re Farepak Food and Gifts Limited (in administration)* (2006) (Chapter 8) and *Farah Constructions Pty Ltd and others* v *Say-Dee Pty Ltd* (2007) (Chapter 13). However, it may have been given a new lease of life by the speech of Lord Scott in *Thorner* v *Major* (see below).

This debate is fundamentally about whether a constructive trust should be tied to equitable principles, albeit functioning as a remedy in one sense as in *Boardman* v *Phipps* [1967] or if it should simply be a general remedy, taking its place alongside damages and injunctions (see Gardner, 2003: 121–127).

Estoppel

KEY DEFINITION: Estoppel

> This arises where one person (the representee) has been led to act on the representation of another (the representor). If so, and if the representee then acts to their detriment on the basis of this promise, then in equity the court may grant the representee a remedy.

Proprietary estoppel and promissory estoppel

Promissory estoppel applies in contractual relationships and essentially prevents a party from going back on a promise. It operates in a defensive mode.

Proprietary estoppel applies in property as well as contractual situations and can, unlike promissory estoppel, give rights where none existed before.

Although you do need to be aware of promissory estoppel proprietary estoppel is more likely to feature in your exam as promissory estoppel is usually examined in contract exams.

Proprietary estoppel

! Don't be tempted to...

Make sure that you can discuss the debate started by Lord Scott in *Yeoman's Row Management Limited* v *Cobbe* (below) on whether estoppel should, in effect, only operate as a defence to an action and not allow an independent right to be asserted. If so there would be no difference between promissory and proprietary estoppel.

Example 9.2

Proprietary estoppel

X owns a piece of land and says to Y: 'You can have it as a market garden'. Y takes over the land and develops it as a market garden but the land is never conveyed to him. X later attempts to turn Y out.

Here there is no deed of conveyance but equity provides that it could be unjust to allow a person in X's position to rely on this fact, so it may be remedied by the doctrine of proprietary estoppel.

EXAM TIP

Note that as estoppel is an example of equity there is a good deal of discretion in this area and it is unwise to come to a black and white conclusion.

The nature of proprietary estoppel has been the subject of two important cases which you must be fully aware of for your exam.

EXAM TIP

You may be able to use these cases as examples of the nature of equity and equitable relief and also in a discussion on unconscionability.

KEY CASE

Yeoman's Row Management Limited v *Cobbe* [2008] UKHL 55

Concerning: estoppel: basic principles

Facts

An oral agreement between the company and Cobbe provided that a block of flats owned by the company would be demolished and Cobbe would apply for planning permission to erect houses in their place with any excess of the proceeds over £24 million shared equally with the company. After planning permission had been obtained the company went back on the oral agreement and demanded more money. Cobbe claimed that the company was estopped from going back on the agreement.

Legal principle

Estoppel did not apply. No specific property right had been promised to Cobbe nor would it be unconscionable for the company to go back on its assurance as Cobbe knew that only a formal contract would be binding.

Thorner v *Major* (2009) UKHL 18

Concerning: estoppel: basic principles

Facts

D had worked at P's farm for no payment from 1976 onwards, and by the 1980s, he had come to hope that he might inherit the farm. No express representation had ever been made, but D relied on various hints and remarks made by P over the years, which he claimed had led him to believe that he was to inherit the farm. In addition, in 1990 P had handed D a bonus notice relating to two policies on P's life, saying 'that's for my death duties'.

Legal principle

The handing over of the bonus notice in 1990 should not be considered alone, and the evidence had demonstrated a continuing pattern of conduct by P for the remaining 15 years of his life sufficient to amount to an estoppel.

Note that Lord Scott in effect proposed that where a future property right (as in *Thorner* v *Major)* was the subject of a representation then the claim should be on the basis of a remedial constructive trust (see above) instead of estoppel as when the promise was made there was no specific property to which it could apply. The other judges however applied proprietary estoppel. See McFarlane (2009) for a discussion of this debate.

 Make your answer stand out

Where there is a claim based on a constructive trust/estoppel it might be appropriate to mention unjust enrichment. See the discussion by Lord Scott in *Yeoman's Row* v *Cobbe* of the possibility of an unjust enrichment claim in that case.

▪ **Chapter summary**: putting it all together

Test yourself

☐ Can you tick all the points from the **revision checklist** at the beginning of this chapter?

☐ Attempt the **sample question** from the beginning of this chapter using the answer guidelines below.

☐ Go to the **companion website** to access more revision support online, including interactive quizzes, sample questions with answer guidelines, 'you be the marker' exercises, flashcards and podcasts you can download.

Answer guidelines

See the essay question at the start of the chapter.

Approaching the question

Trustees are in a fiduciary position: you will earn marks for a careful and clear explanation of the term 'fiduciary'.

Important points to include

▪ Osbert has taken advantage of his position to purchase shares and obtain an appointment as fee paying director.

▪ Apply case law: *Keech* v *Sandford*, and especially *Boardman* v *Phipps*. Need to contrast these with *Queensland Mines Ltd* v *Hudson*.

▪ It is almost certain that Osbert will hold on constructive trust.

▪ Will the court allow 'liberal payment' as in *Boardman*? Probably not as here Osbert's conduct is a clearer breach than that of *Boardman*.

 Make your answer stand out

A thorough knowledge of *Boardman* v *Phipps* and an ability to see the contrast with *Queensland Mines Ltd* v *Hudson* is essential. Research detail on other cases.

READ TO IMPRESS

Conaglen (2009) 'Fiduciary Regulation of Conflicts Between Duties', 125 LQR 111.

Dixon, M. (2005) 'Resulting and Constructive Trusts of Land; the Mist Descends and Rises', 69 Conv. 79.

Dixon, M. (2007) 'The never-ending story – co-ownership after *Stack* v *Dowden*', Conv. 456.

Finn, P.D. (1985) *Essays in Equity*, North Ryde, N.S.W.: Law Book Company.

Gardner, S. (1993) 'Rethinking Family Property', 109 LQR 263.

Gardner, S. (2003) *An Introduction to the Law of Trusts*, 2nd edn, Oxford: Oxford University Press.

Koh, J. (2003) 'Once a Director, Always a Fiduciary?' 62 CLJ 403.

McFarlane (2009) 'Apocalypse averted: proprietary estoppel in the House of Lords', 125 LQR 535.

Millett, P. (1998) 'Restitution and Constructive Trusts', 114 LQR 399.

Moffatt, G. (2009) *Trusts Law: Text and Materials*, 5th edn, Cambridge: Cambridge University Press.

Rotherham, C. (2004) 'The Property Rights of Unmarried Cohabitees: a Case for Reform', 68 Conv. 268. An excellent general survey.

Swadling, W. (2007) 'The Common Intention Constructive Trust in the House of Lords: an Opportunity Missed', LQR 511.

Tan, D.(1995) 'The fiduciary as an accordion term: can the Crown play a different tune?' 69 ALJ 440.

NOTES

NOTES

NOTES

10

Charitable trusts

Revision checklist

Essential points you should know:

- [ ] what is meant by charitable purposes?
- [ ] what is meant by public benefit and what this means in the context of each head of charity
- [ ] charitable trusts must be exclusively charitable
- [ ] the scope of the *cy-près* doctrine and the position when it does not apply

■ Topic map

Advantages of
charitable status

Forms of charitable
organisations

Charitable purposes

Public benefit

Must be exclusively
charitable

Failure of charitable
and non-charitable gifts

A printable version of this topic map is available from www.pearsoned.co.uk/lawexpress

▉Introduction

This is one of the most common areas for questions in an equity exam paper.

It lends itself to both essay and problem questions neither of which are too difficult but they do require a good knowledge of case law. It is essential that you are aware of the main provisions of the Charities Act 2006 which brought the first major change in the statute law on this subject since the Statute of Charitable Uses Act 1601. You also need to be up to date on the current debate on what constitutes public benefit. The website of the Charity Commission (www.charity-commission.gov.uk) is an excellent place to start your research. Do keep up with the implementation timetable of the Act – also available on this website.

ASSESSMENT ADVICE

Essay questions There are two main possible essay questions:

1 Essay questions on the requirement of public benefit.
2 A more general essay question on the Charities Act 2006, possibly looking at the place of charities in society in the light of the changes made by the Act. You do need to look at the background to the Act and be able to discuss the main controversial issues (e.g. the extent to which public benefit should be required for a charitable trust).

Problem questions There are two main possible problem questions:

1 Problem questions on whether particular objects of a trust are charitable.
2 Problem questions on the failure of charitable gifts.

The first area is the most likely and it will require you to know and be able to apply the relevant part of the Charities Act and also to discuss the extent to which cases decided under the previous law are still relevant. Select some cases and test them against the new law.

Note very precisely what the question asks you to do. It may either ask you to advise on whether the gift (often in a will) is charitable or to advise on the validity of the gift. If it is the latter then, if you decide that the gift cannot be charitable, you need to ask if it could be valid as a private trust or, possibly, if it comes under one of the cases where non-charitable trusts are valid.

■ Sample question

Could you answer this question? Below is a typical problem question that could arise on this topic. Guidelines on answering the question are included at the end of the chapter, while a sample essay question and guidance on tackling it can be found on the companion website.

PROBLEM QUESTION

Albert, by will, left the following bequests:

(a) £10,000 to the Worcester Women's Benevolent Society which provides grants to elderly women in Worcester who are in need.

(b) £15,000 to the Faith Society which welcomes those of any faith or none to join them in their quest for spiritual enlightenment.

(c) £20,000 to provide scholarships to enable children resident in Worcester to attend university, preference to be given to children of workers employed in the porcelain industry in Worcester.

(d) The residue of his property on trust to be used for such charitable, humanitarian or benevolent causes as his trustees may select.

Can you advise Albert's trustees on the validity of these gifts?

■ Advantages of charitable status

This topic can appear in an essay question and you should be prepared to discuss it under two heads:

1 legal
2 fiscal, i.e. taxation.

You are unlikely to be asked a detailed question on the fiscal advantages and so concentrate on the legal ones:

1 Trusts for non-charitable purposes are generally void (see Chapter 4) as there is no one to enforce them, but the Attorney General can enforce charitable trusts and, in practice, the Charity Commissioners police the charity sector. There is scope here for a good answer which thinks laterally by linking material on both types of purpose trusts – charitable and non-charitable – and compares them from the point of view of enforceability.

2 The requirement of certainty of objects does not apply to charitable trusts. Once again impress the examiner with lateral thinking and draw a comparison with private trusts.

See, for example, *McPhail* v *Doulton* [1971] in Chapter 3.

Rule against perpetuity

It is worth taking time to be absolutely clear about what the rule against perpetuities means as very few students do so and it will be a real plus point for you in the exam!

Revise the Rule now – see Chapter 4 which deals with it in another context and so knowledge of the rule will be useful in two possible exam questions.

However, having revised the Rule, you then need to point out that as far as charities are concerned a gift over from one charity to another which takes place *beyond* the perpetuity period is not affected by the rule.

Example 10.1

In his will Jack leaves all his estate to Hanbury School, a registered charity, but provides that if the school shall ever cease to exist then any remaining funds from the estate not used shall go to the Hospital of St John. Clearly this may take place long beyond the new 125-year perpetuity period. Even so, the gift is valid.

Take some time to master the above point. Greater detail will not be needed: just clarity about the precise point!

Forms of charitable organisations

This is really just background detail but it will stop you making fundamental errors! Although charity law is a part of the law of trusts (because charities were enforced by equity and not the common law) a charity can exist as:

- a trust

- a company

- an unincorporated association, i.e. a body which is not a company and which has technically no legal existence – see Chapter 4 for more on this.

Definition of charity

Three basic tests for charitable status exist (see Figure 10.1).

EXAM TIP

Make sure that in a problem question you apply each of these tests to each situation.

Figure 10.1

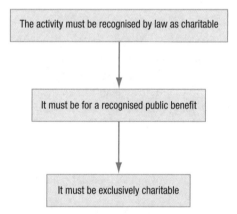

The activity must be recognised by law as charitable

It must be for a recognised public benefit

It must be exclusively charitable

Charitable purposes recognised by law

Section 2(2) of the Charities Act 2006 sets out the charitable purposes recognised by law. This Act fundamentally overhauled charity law.

The following sections refer to paragraphs of s. 2(2).

(a) Prevention or relief of poverty

Re Coulthurst [1951] Ch 661 (HC)

Concerning: meaning of 'poverty' in charity law

Facts

The facts of this case do not aid an understanding of the legal principle.

Legal principle

Evershed MR said that 'poverty does not mean destitution ... it may not be unfairly paraphrased as meaning persons who have to 'go short''.

Re Niyazi's Will Trusts [1978] 3 All ER 785 (HC)

Concerning: application of the meaning of poverty in charity law

Facts

A gift was left as a contribution to the cost of building a 'working men's hostel'.

Legal principle

This was charitable, even though there was no express limitation to those who were poor as the words 'working men' and 'hostel' indicated those with a lower income.

(b) Advancement of education

Exam questions often deal with trusts for research: are they educational?

Re Hopkins' Will Trusts [1965] Ch 669 (HC)

Concerning: meaning of education

Facts

A trust for the promotion of research into finding the Bacon–Shakespeare manuscripts was held charitable.

▶

Legal principle

Education must be used in a wide sense and extends beyond teaching. Research must either:

- be of educational value to the researcher, or
- pass into the store of educational material or improve the sum of communicable knowledge.

(c) Advancement of religion

KEY CASE

Thornton v *Howe* (1862) 31 Beav 14 Ct of Chan

Concerning: trusts for the advancement of religion

Facts

A trust to promote the writings of Joanna Southcote, who founded a small sect and who proclaimed that she was with child by the Holy Ghost and would give birth to a second Messiah, was held charitable.

Legal principle

Provided that the trust exists for the advancement of religion the court will not say that it fails as a charity because it disapproves of its beliefs. However, note the comments of Goff J in *Church of Scientology* v *Kaufman* (1973) below.

 Make your answer stand out

The Charities Act contains an extended definition of religion to include non-deity and multi-deity groups. To what extent will this change the law, if at all? Read *Hansard*, 3 February and 10 February 1988, which details debates on the decision to refuse registration as a charity to the Unification Church (The Moonies). Harding (2008) has an excellent discussion in the light of the requirements of the Charities Act 2006. See also Iwobi (2009) who also discusses (at p. 644) the compatibility of the charitable conception of religion with rights under the ECHR, an interesting angle which could add value to an answer.

This is a good point to note that the courts do make judgments, assisted by expert evidence, on the value of the trust in, for example, educational or religious terms. An example is Goff J in *Church of Scientology* v *Kaufman* (1973) who described the objects of the church as 'pernicious nonsense'.

Heads of charity

The new heads under the Charities Act 2006 are as follows. (The following list begins at (d) as (a) poverty, (b) education and (c) religion have been discussed above.)

(d) Advancement of health or the saving of lives.

(e) Advancement of citizenship or community development.

(f) Advancement of the arts, culture, heritage or science.

(g) Advancement of amateur sport. (Note that sport only qualifies if it involves physical exertion.)

(h) Advancement of human rights, conflict resolution or reconciliation or the promotion of religious or racial harmony or equality and diversity. (See below under the discussion of political trusts.)

(i) Advancement of environmental protection or improvement.

(j) Relief of those in need by reason of youth, old age, ill health, disability, financial hardship or other disadvantage.

(k) Advancement of animal welfare.

(l) The promotion of the efficiency of the armed forces of the Crown.

(m) Other purposes currently recognised as charitable and any new charitable purposes which are similar to another charitable purpose.

In an exam question on the changes in the definition of charity in the Charities Act 2006 you should point out four things:

1 Many of these objects simply make a particular object specifically charitable when it was included under the general fourth head in the previous law on what constituted charitable status. This had the general title of trusts for other purposes beneficial to the community and included, for example, animal welfare which is now head (k) under the Charities Act 2006 (see above).

2 In some cases the object formed part of an existing object and is now on its own: for example, advancement of the arts, heritage or science would previously have come mainly under education.

3 In some cases the new charitable objects may go further than the existing ones (e.g. promotion of amateur sport).

4 In other cases the law is brought into line with the current practice of the Charity Commission (e.g. new definition of religion, etc.).

Make sure that in a problem question you apply each of these tests to each situation.

When revising do not just memorise the new heads of charity but instead do two things:

1 Look at each head in the light of the above bullet points.
2 Do some deeper research into perhaps four of them: there will not be time in an exam question to say something useful about them all.

The Charities Act also preserves some other existing charitable purposes, for example, under the Recreational Charities Act 1958, which makes recreational *facilities* charitable.

If you see a mention of, for example, village halls and sports centres in a question then it is likely that the Recreational Charities Act 1958 will be relevant.

Requirement of a recognised public benefit

In order to be charitable the objects of a trust must be for the benefit of a section of the public. A trust set up for the education of named children, for example, would not be charitable (*Re Compton* (1945)).

Summary

The Charities Act 2006 has changed the law in this area and you must stress three points in the exam:

1 Section 3(2) provides that there is no longer any presumption of public benefit.
2 Section 3(3) in effect provides that the existing case law on what is understood to constitute public benefit shall continue to have effect. This, of course, is subject to s. 3(2) above.
3 Section 4(1) provides that the Charity Commission must issue guidance on what constitutes public benefit. This cannot change the law but it does give evidence of what the Charity Commission's views on public benefit are, especially where there is no longer any presumption of public benefit and so any case law on this particular point is no longer applicable. The key principles set out by the Charity Commission are shown below.

Abolition of presumption of public benefit

This is where the Charities Act 2006 makes a major change and you must be aware of it for the exam:

Under the previous law:

■ The advancement of education and religion were presumed in principle to benefit the public although actual benefit still needed to be proved.

■ There was hardly any requirement that trusts for the relief of poverty had to be for the public benefit. See *Dingle* v *Turner* (1972) for an example of how the law used to be applied.

■ Public benefit had to be proved in charities under what was the fourth head. (This was a general head defined as other purposes beneficial to the community.)

Under the Charities Act 2006:

■ Public benefit must be proved in all cases and it is no longer assumed that education and religion are by themselves beneficial to the public. In addition trusts for the relief of poverty will in future have to prove public benefit.

EXAM TIP

Do some research on the effect which this will have. Independent schools are a good example.

Key principles

The Charity Commission has set out two key principles of public benefit which are essential to learn for exams:

1 There must be an identifiable benefit(s).
  (a) It must be clear what the benefits are
  (b) The benefits must be related to the aims
  (c) Benefits must be balanced against any detriment or harm.
2 Benefit must be to the public, or a section of the public.
  (a) The beneficiaries must be appropriate to the aims
  (b) Where benefit is to a section of the public, the opportunity to benefit must not be unreasonably restricted:
    ■ by geographical or other restrictions
    ■ by ability to pay any fees charged.
  (c) People in poverty must not be excluded from the opportunity to benefit.
  (d) Any private benefits must be incidental.

The Charity Commission website has more information on these principles and also on the supplementary guidance which has been issued on public benefit and particular types of charity (e.g. education, religion, prevention or relief of poverty and public benefit and fee charging). It is absolutely essential that you keep up to date with what is happening here.

You will find the following cases on public benefit decided under the old law still useful as existing case law will be used to decide if there is public benefit but you must relate them to the above principles.

KEY CASE

Oppenheim v *Tobacco Securities Trust Co. Ltd* [1951] AC 297 (HL)

Concerning: public benefit in trusts for the advancement of education

Facts

A trust was set up for the education of children of employees or ex-employees of British American Tobacco.

Legal principle

This was not charitable as there was a personal connection: all the beneficiaries were connected with the same company.

 Make your answer stand out

The decision in *Oppenheim* has been criticised, especially given that the company had over 100,000 employees and so the potential beneficiaries were a very large number. Read Lord McDermott's noteable dissenting judgment to give you another viewpoint on what the test should be on what can constitute the public or a section of it. This will add to your marks.

KEY CASE

Re Koettgen's Will Trusts [1954] Ch 252 (HC)

Concerning: public benefit where there was a preference for a limited class

Facts

A trust for commercial education provided that preference should be given to employees of a named company of up to 75 per cent of income.

Legal principle

This was charitable as a preference for a private group does not necessarily mean that there is no public benefit.

This case often comes up in problem questions and you should be familiar with the facts, as the problem will have slightly different ones. It is likely that a trust which provided that a greater proportion of the income than in this case would go to the preferential class (e.g. 85 per cent) would not be valid.

KEY CASE

Gilmour v *Coates* [1949] AC 426 (HL)

Concerning: requirement of public benefit in trusts for the advancement of religion

Facts

A gift was left by a will to a convent of nuns who were strictly cloistered and who had no contact with the outside world.

Legal principle

This was not charitable as there was no evidence of public benefit. The prayers of the nuns could not be said to benefit the public as there was no proof of this.

 Make your answer stand out

The attitude of the courts to public benefit had caused controversy and it has been suggested that at times it was too strict. Read Moffat (2009: 1006–1023) which has an excellent critique of the law. Look also at the Reports of the Charity Commission – available on its website.

Political trusts

A trust which has objects which are political cannot be charitable. The reason is that it is not for the courts to decide if what may be a controversial purpose should be for the public benefit given the tax advantages which charities have.

KEY CASE

McGovern v *Attorney-General* [1981] 3 All ER 493 (HC)

Concerning: trusts for political objects

Facts

Amnesty International set up a trust with these objects:

(a) relief of needy persons who were, or might be, prisoners of conscience
(b) attempting to secure their release
(c) abolition of torture or other inhumane methods of treatment or punishment
(d) research into human rights.

Legal principle

Objects (a) and (d) were charitable but (b) and (c) were political as they were designed to change the policies of governments and/or change the law. Thus the trust was not charitable.

 Make your answer stand out

This case led to much discussion (e.g. see Chesterman (1999) and subsequent reports of the Charity Commissioners, in particular the most recent guidance issued by the Charity Commissioners). Research the extent to which the new head of charity (h) (human rights etc.) will enable charities to engage in activities (b) and (c) in *McGovern* (above).

■ Must be exclusively charitable

A gift cannot be charitable if one or more of its purposes are not charitable.

Always check for this last requirement in an exam question: it is sometimes forgotten! A good case on this point is *McGovern* v *A–G* [1981] (above).

KEY CASE

Chichester Diocesan Fund and Board of Finance Inc. v *Simpson* (1944) AC 341 (HL)

Concerning: requirement that a trust must be exclusively charitable

Facts

A trust was established for 'charitable or benevolent objects'.

> **Legal principle**
>
> It was not exclusively charitable as the words 'or benevolent' implied that the trust existed for objects which were not charitable.

EXAM TIP

This case often appears in exam questions and there may be a variation to 'charitable and benevolent objects'. This will make the trust charitable as the word 'or' implies two objects, one of which (benevolent) is not charitable, but 'and' implies just one, which is charitable. However, it must be said that such nit picking does equity little credit!

EXAM TIP

In a problem question on charities watch carefully for what the question asks you to do:

- Advise whether the gifts are valid charitable gifts
- Advise whether the gifts are valid.

In this second case you will gain extra marks by looking at whether the gift could take effect as a valid private trust or perhaps a valid non-charitable purpose trust (see Chapter 4) if it is not charitable.

■ Failure of charitable and non-charitable gifts

A gift to a particular body, whether a charity or not, may fail because, for example,

- the body no longer exists
- it had never existed
- it had been amalgamated with another body.

In these cases, we need to decide where the gift goes to. It could be held on a resulting trust for the donor, or their estate. However, the law is reluctant, especially where the gift was intended for charitable purposes, to allow it to go away from the charitable sector, and so it is possible for the gift to be applied for similar charitable purposes under the *cy-près* doctrine.

'So near'.

EXAM TIP

This usually appears as a separate exam question and is likely to be a problem. It may involve gifts for non-charitable purposes as well, which is why they are also dealt with here. You may get what is in effect a two-part question: the first part asks you if the gift is charitable and then you are asked to deal with the position where it has failed.

Failure of charitable gifts

Example 10.2

In his will Richard leaves £10,000 to his old school, Wigorn College. However, at the date of his death, the school had ceased to exist. Advise the trustees of Richard's will.

The first question is whether the gift was for charitable purposes. The answer seems to be yes, although extra marks here for mentioning that under the Charities Act the public benefit requirement is tighter.

Assuming that it is, you need to discuss *cy-près* application. This will allow the gift to be applied for purposes *cy-près* (so near) (i.e. as near as possible) to the original purposes (see Figure 10.2).

Figure 10.2

Gift by will of £10,000

Initial charitable gift but has failed

Result: May be possible to apply it *cy-près*

The result is that, returning to the example, two requirements must be satisfied:

1 The donor (Richard) must have shown a *general charitable intention*, i.e. not just to benefit that school but educational charity in a more general way (e.g. see *Re Rymer* (1895)). Note also *Re Harwood* (1936): easier to find a general charitable intention where the body had never existed at all.

2   The gift has failed within the meaning of the Charities Act 1993, s. 13 (as amended by the Charities Act 2006).

Suppose that this is not so. Then there is another possibility: has the school amalgamated with another school so that that school is carrying on its purposes? If so, then it may claim the gift (see *Re Faraker* (1912)).

If the problem is that there is no general charitable intention then *Re Slevin* (1891) may come to the rescue as shown in Figure 10.3.

Figure 10.3

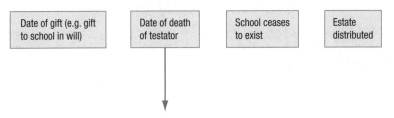

At the date this gift has been given to charity and so any lack of general charitable intention is irrelevant: *cy-près* application will follow

Thus, in the above example, if the school existed at the date of Richard's death but before the £10,000 was paid over, no general charitable intention need be shown for *cy-près* to apply. This is known as subsequent failure.

The above discussion has assumed that the school operates as a company, which is likely because of legal liabilities. Suppose that it was an unincorporated association?

REVISION NOTE

Remember that these do not exist in law as such and this can have unfortunate consequences which we considered in Chapter 4.

However, if the gift fails as the association ceases to exist then unincorporated association status is a positive advantage as the gift was never made to the association anyway. So, provided that its purposes are still continuing, the gift can go to a body which is carrying them on. (See *Re Finger's Will Trusts* [1972].)

Failure of non-charitable gifts

Suppose that we are not dealing with a charitable gift at all. This will be so where the purposes are not charitable and this usually arises in two situations in exams:

Situation one	Situation two
Donations are made to a disaster fund which turns out not to be charitable (e.g. see *Re Gillingham Bus Disaster Fund* [1959]). A surplus remains.	A social club is wound up. (Revision point: why isn't it charitable?) What happens to the surplus? Two possibilities:
In *Re Gillingham* it was held that it went on a resulting trust for the donors, even if they could not be found.	1 It goes to the members – see e.g. *Re Bucks Constabulary Fund (No. 2)* (1979)
	2 It goes to the Crown as **bona vacantia** – see *Re West Sussex Constabulary Fund* [1970].

Section 14 of the Charities Act 2006 allows a charity appeal to state that if the charitable purposes fail, gifts will be applied *cy-près*.

 Make your answer stand out

This area is unsatisfactory and you should consider the alternative possibilities. For a really good mark, read Chambers (1997: 61–67) who looks at all of the cases and analyses them from the point of view of resulting trusts.

■Chapter summary: putting it all together

Test yourself

- ☐ Can you tick all the points from the **revision checklist** at the beginning of this chapter?
- ☐ Attempt the **sample question** from the beginning of this chapter using the answer guidelines below.
- ☐ Go to the **companion website** to access more revision support online, including interactive quizzes, sample questions with answer guidelines, 'you be the marker' exercises, flashcards and podcasts you can download.

Answer guidelines

See the problem question at the start of the chapter.

Approaching the question

In each case, ask three questions:

1. Is the gift for charitable purposes?
2. If so, is there sufficient public benefit?
3. If so, is it exclusively charitable?

Remember: unless it is absolutely certain that the gift does not satisfy 1 you should go on to consider 2, and the same applies to 2 and 3.

Important points to include

- (a) Gift may be for the relief of poverty but is there a public benefit?
- (b) Is the society for the advancement of religion? If not, could it come under other heads?
- (c) The purpose is educational but a public benefit? Look at *Oppenheim* and *Re Koettgen*.
- (d) Exclusively charitable? *Chichester Diocesan Fund* v *Simpson*. Humanitarian?

▶

Make your answer stand out

In (b) adopt an imaginative approach to where the purpose could fit in.

In (c) exhibit a clear knowledge of the facts of *Re Koettgen* and knowledge of critical approaches to the law (e.g. Lord McDermott's dissenting judgment in *Oppenheim*).

READ TO IMPRESS

Chambers, R. (1997) *Resulting Trusts*, Oxford: Oxford University Press.

Chesterman, M. (1999) 'Foundations of Charity Law in the New Welfare State', 62 MLR 333.

Hackney J. (2008) 'Charities and public benefit', 124 LQR 347.

Harding, M. (2008) 'Trusts for Religious Purposes and the Question of Public Benefit', 71 MLR 159.

Iwobi A. (2009) 'Out with the old, in with the new: religion, charitable status and the Charities Act 2006' 29 LS 619.

Moffat, G. (2009) *Trusts Law and Materials*, 5th edn, Cambridge: Cambridge University Press.

NOTES

NOTES

11

Trusteeship

Revision checklist

Essential points you should know:

- [ ] the rules on appointment, retirement and removal of trustees (in brief)
- [ ] the meaning of the term 'fiduciary' and its implications for trustees
- [ ] the distinction between duties and powers of trustees
- [ ] the main duties and powers
- [ ] the extent to which trustees may delegate
- [ ] the extent to which the trust instrument may exclude the liability of trustees
- [ ] situations when the terms of a trust may be varied

■ Topic map

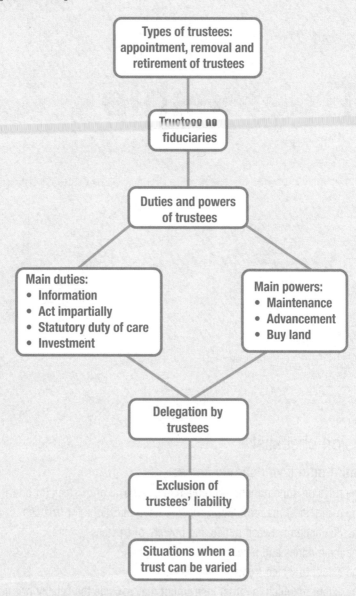

Types of trustees:
appointment, removal and
retirement of trustees

Trustees as
fiduciaries

Duties and powers
of trustees

Main duties:
- Information
- Act impartially
- Statutory duty of care
- Investment

Main powers:
- Maintenance
- Advancement
- Buy land

Delegation by
trustees

Exclusion of
trustees' liability

Situations when a
trust can be varied

A printable version of this topic map is available from www.pearsoned.co.uk/lawexpress

◼Introduction

The topic of trusteeship is not a difficult one but it does involve a good deal of material.

It is a practical area and so it is a good idea to familiarise yourself with an actual trust instrument to see what one looks like and to be able to identify the main types of clauses. (There is one on the website for this book.) There is also an interesting shift in the case law to recognising different obligations owed by fiduciaries in some types of commercial relationships from those traditionally owed. See the cases below on exclusion of liability. Note that this is not the only chapter in which trustees are considered: Chapter 9 also contains material on the fiduciary duties of trustees and you should make sure that you are familiar with it before starting this chapter.

REVISION NOTE

Refer back to Chapter 9 and check cases such as *Keech* v *Sandford* (1726) and *Boardman* v *Phipps* 9 sub (1967). Questions on trustees often link with constructive trusts.

ASSESSMENT ADVICE

Essay questions This is a likely area for an essay question with possibilities of questions on:

- the extent of the duties of trustees, of which an example is set out below
- the fiduciary principle, where you can use your knowledge of the constructive trust cases
- the changes made by the Trustee Act 2000: this is getting a bit old hat now but examiners may still ask it
- the relationship between the statutory duties and powers of trustees and those in a trust instrument.

Problem questions Questions are likely on the application of a range of duties and powers. For example, a common question examines powers of maintenance and advancement, or investment possibly combined with delegation. Do remember that the Trustee Act 1925 applies to maintenance and advancement. ▶

Other areas are governed by the Trustee Act 2000. Again a question may bring in the scenario in *Boardman* v *Phipps* (1967) and link it with other topics which are governed by the Trustee Act 2000 (e.g. trustees' right to remuneration). In all questions identify at the start whether a duty and/or a power is involved and state clearly the different principles applicable to the relevant one.

■ Sample question

Could you answer this question? Below is a typical problem question that could arise on this topic. Guidelines on answering the question are included at the end of the chapter, whilst a sample essay question and guidance on tackling it can be found on the companion website.

PROBLEM QUESTION

Arthur died in 2004. His will appointed Steve and Bryn as trustees of a fund worth £500,000 to hold for the benefit of Arthur's children, Kate (aged 25), Sue (aged 21) and Mary (aged 16), contingent on them reaching the age of 30.

You are asked to advise the trustees on the following:

(a) Kate, who works in an investment bank, has told them that it would be an excellent idea to invest the bulk of the fund in a company specialising in property developments in France as 'there is certain to be a property boom there next year'. If the trustees hand over the money to Kate then she is prepared to take care of the investment details.

(b) Steve thinks that it would be a good idea to invest some of the money in a small private company run by Terry, a friend of his. Terry has offered to appoint Steve a paid director if this happens.

(c) Sue would like £70,000 of 'her money' to be paid to her now as she wishes to set up a hairdressing business. She has recently qualified as a hairdresser.

(d) Mary would like the sum of £500 to be paid to her each year so that she can receive singing lessons in Milan.

Appointment of trustees

It is unlikely that an exam question will ask you to deal with this area in detail. However, you may get a question on the relationship between the powers contained in the trust instrument and statutory powers so this area gives you a useful illustration.

Appointment of trustees is normally made in the first instance by the settlor or testator in the instrument or will which creates the trust. What happens later when existing trustees need to be replaced? This is where the statutory power in s. 36(1) of the Trustee Act 1925 (TA 1925) comes in, as it lists eight cases where trustees who, for example, die, wish to be discharged, etc. can be replaced by the remaining trustees. In addition, appointment also brings in the other element, that of control by the court as under s. 41, TA 1925 the court can appoint new trustees where it is 'impracticable or inexpedient to do so without the assistance of the court'.

Retirement and removal of trustees

This also involves the relationship between the statutory powers and the trust instrument although in the case of removal it is more likely that this will be done by the court. Retirement of trustees is governed by s. 39, TA 1925 and removal is governed by the general powers of the court.

Trustees as fiduciaries

The topic of trustees as fiduciaries is considered in Chapter 9.

REVISION NOTE

Go back to Chapter 9 and check that you are clear what a fiduciary is and look at cases where trustees have been held liable as constructive trustees as they have been in breach of their fiduciary duty. This is also a good example of where you can use the same cases to illustrate more than one point of law.

- The fiduciary nature of trusteeship prevents payment of trustees unless authorised by the trust instrument or by statute – the relevant one here is s. 29 Trustee Act 2000.

- Trustees are also not allowed to purchase trust property but an exceptional case where they were is *Holder* v *Holder* [1968].

Duties and powers of trustees

The fundamental duty of the trustee is the fiduciary duty (above) but there are specific duties and powers:

- A *duty* must be exercised, although the trustee has a discretion as to precisely how it is exercised (e.g. a trustee has a duty to invest but a discretion in what to invest in).

- A *power* is discretionary but if it is a discretionary trust the trustees may be obliged to exercise a discretion.

The courts can interfere in the exercise of trustees' powers if they have acted in bad faith (*Klug* v *Klug*) but contrast *Tempest* v *Lord Camoys* where no bad faith was shown and so the court did not interfere. Nor can the courts require trustees to give reasons for their decisions (*Re Beloved Wilkes' Charity*), but if they do give reasons for their decisions then the court may investigate them (*Klug* v *Klug*).

What is the position if trustees make a mistake? The leading case is *Re Hastings-Bass (1975)*. *Sieff* v *Fox (2005)* is the most recent explanation of the principle set out in it.

KEY CASE

Sieff v Fox (2005) EWHC 1312

Concerning: application of the principle in Re Hastings-Bass

Facts

Trustees, acting on mistaken legal advice, made a decision resulting in a charge to Capital Gains Tax of around £1m. The decision was set aside.

Legal principle

Lloyd J. stated that: 'Where trustees act under a discretion given to them by the terms of the trust, in circumstances in which they are free to decide whether or not to exercise that discretion, but the effect of the exercise is different from that which they intended, *the court will interfere with their action if it is clear that they would not have acted as they did had they not failed to take into account considerations which they ought to have taken into account, or taken into account considerations which they ought not to have taken into account.*' (Italics added.)

Make your answer stand out

This is a topical area worth looking at for exams. See Mitchell (2006) and Nolan and Conaglen (2006). Look also at *Abacus Trust Co. (Isle of Man) Ltd.* v *NSPCC* (2001) and compare the approach in that case with that in *Stieff* v *Fox*. Add to your marks by mentioning the position of Scottish law on control of trustees. See Francis (2008).

Relationship between powers in the trust instrument and statutory powers

The legislation on trustees' powers operates in default of any provision in the trust instrument to the contrary (see s. 69(2), Trustee Act 1925). This is a useful point to explore in an essay question and is also relevant in problems (e.g. on powers of maintenance and advancement – see below).

Main duties of trustees

The duty to give information

The extent of the duty to give information to the beneficiaries is somewhat unclear and would form good material for an essay question on the extent to which trustees are accountable to the beneficiaries. There has been a shift from the approach in *Re Londonderry's Settlement* [1965], which emphasised that beneficiaries are allowed to see documents which contain information about the trust that the beneficiaries are entitled to know and in which the beneficiaries have a proprietary interest. In *Schmidt* v *Rosewood Trust Ltd* (2003) the court emphasised that the issue is the requirement for the court to supervise the trust.

Duty to act impartially

KEY CASE

Howe v *Earl of Dartmouth* (1802) 7 Ves 137 Chan

Concerning: duties of trustees between a life tenant and a remainderman

Facts

The facts of this case do not aid an understanding of the legal principle.

Legal principle

The trustee must act impartially and so must strike a balance between the interests of the life tenant (income required) and the remainderman (preservation of capital required).

Statutory duty of care

This was introduced by the Trustee Act 2000 and it is vital that you read the background to this Act. The fundamental reason why it was introduced was that the duties of trustees were governed mainly by nineteenth century case law which was quite out of date.

KEY STATUTE

Trustee Act 2000, s. 1

A trustee shall exercise such care as is reasonable having regard in particular to:

(a) any special knowledge or experience which he has or holds himself out as having

(b) if he acts in the course of a business or profession, any special knowledge or experience which is reasonable to expect of a person acting in that business or profession.

The statutory duty of care applies to:

- investment
- acquisition of land
- appointment of agents
- insurance
- compounding of liabilities
- reversionary interests, valuations and audit.

With regard to investment the following are relevant:

KEY STATUTE

Trustee Act 2000

Section 3

A trustee may make any investment that he could make if he was absolutely entitled under the trust.

Section 4

The standard investment criteria when investing are:

(a) the suitability to the trust of particular investments

(b) the need for diversification of investments, so far as this is appropriate.

> **Section 5**
>
> A trustee must obtain and consider advice about the way in which the power of investment should be exercised. Note that s. 5 defines what this is and when trustees are relieved of this duty.

Cases on investment may still be useful, even if decided under the previous law (e.g. *Cowan* v *Scargill* [1985]).

Main powers of trustees

Powers of **maintenance** and **advancement**.

> **KEY DEFINITION: Maintenance**
>
> Payment of income to beneficiaries before they are entitled.

> **KEY DEFINITION: Advancement**
>
> Payment of capital to beneficiaries before they are entitled.

These often come up in problem questions and Figure 11.1 shows a flow chart for answering them.

> **KEY CASE**
>
> *Re Kershaw's Trusts* (1868) LR 6 Eq 322 (HC)
>
> *Concerning: meaning of advancement*
>
> **Facts**
>
> An advancement was sought to enable the beneficiary's husband to set up in business and so prevent the family separating.
>
> **Legal principle**
>
> An advancement would be made. The term advancement has a wider meaning than just financial benefit.

Figure 11.1

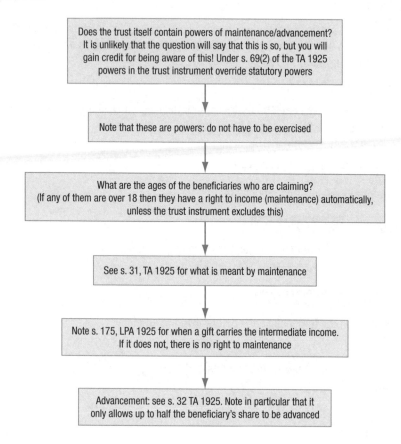

Power to buy land

This is contained in s. 8, TA 2000 and gives trustees very wide powers to buy land.

Delegation by trustees

The power of trustees to delegate is contained in the following:

KEY STATUTE

Trustee Act 2000, s. 11

This allows trustees to delegate all functions except:

- decisions on distribution of assets
- decisions on whether to pay fees or other payments out of income or capital
- appointment of new trustees
- power to sub-delegate.

Liability for the acts of agents is now governed by the statutory duty of care in s. 1, TA 2000 (above).

Exclusion of trustees' liability

KEY CASE

Armitage v *Nurse* [1998] Ch 221 (HC)

Concerning: extent to which trustees can exclude liability

Facts

The trust excluded the liability of the trustees for loss or damage unless caused by the actual fraud of the trustees.

Legal principle

This was upheld.

> ✓ Make your answer stand out
>
> There is a view that trustee exclusion clauses have gone too far (e.g. see McCormack (1998) and *Citibank NA* v *MIBA Assurance SA* (2006).
>
> In *Australian Securities and Investments Commission* v *Citigroup Global Markets Australia Pty Ltd* (2007) an investment bank which advised on a takeover bid stipulated that it was not retained as a fiduciary. This was held to eliminate any liability by the bank when it traded in the shares of the company which its client proposed to take over. The case is also interesting as Jacobsen J distinguished between fiduciaries *per se* (i.e. of the kind this book has been discussing) and where there is a fiduciary relationship arising out of a specific relationship, as here (see Getzler (2008)).

■ Situations where a trust can be varied

Variation of trusts broadly means when a trustee or beneficiary wants to change the terms of the trust. Exams will focus mainly on how a trust can be varied under the Variation of Trusts Act 1958 (VTA) which gives the courts a *general* power to vary trusts, but you need to be aware of other situations where a trust can be varied to add depth to your answer.

Variation by trustees and beneficiaries

- Trustees under the trust instrument – this is unlikely to figure in the exam in detail.
- Beneficiaries under the Rule in *Saunders* v *Vautier* (1841). This usually amounts to termination of the whole trust.

Variation by the court

- Miscellaneous powers Section 57, Trustee Act 1925 – this allows the court to confer extra powers in the management and administration of the trust. A good instance is wider investment powers, although now that these have been increased (see s. 3, Trustee Act 2000 in Chapter 11) this will not be needed so often.
- Emergency powers come under the inherent jurisdiction of the court: one example is where emergency action is needed to save a building from collapse.

You must point out that the above powers do not help where the parties wish to vary the actual terms of the trust (e.g. to vary the actual beneficial interests).

- Under the VTA. This gives the court a general power to vary the beneficial interests under a trust, unlike in the above situations. The court's approval is needed and in an exam question you may be asked to decide if the court should do so. Good cases to include are: *Re Weston's Settlements* [1969] *Re CL* [1969] and *Re Remnant's Settlement Trusts* [1970].

■Chapter summary: putting it all together

Test yourself

☐ Can you tick all the points from the **revision checklist** at the beginning of this chapter?

☐ Attempt the **sample question** from the beginning of this chapter using the answer guidelines below.

☐ Go to the **companion website** to access more revision support online, including interactive quizzes, sample questions with answer guidelines, 'you be the marker' exercises, flashcards and podcasts you can download.

Answer guidelines

See the problem question at the start of this chapter.

Approaching the question

This question requires you to look carefully at the duties and powers of trustees but also to use material from Chapter 9 on fiduciaries and personal liabilities of beneficiaries – Chapter 12. This is a common overlap between subject areas. You should say that you assume that any trust instrument has not altered the duties and powers of the trustees.

Important points to include

(a) Begin with s. 1, TA 2000 (duty of care) and consider this in the light of s. 3 (general powers of investment) and s. 4 (criteria when investing). Trustees can take advice from others (see s. 11, TA 2000) but is this a wise decision here? Note also that Kate is a beneficiary. See Personal Liability of Beneficiary, Chapter 12. ▶

(b) Possible conflict of interest, *Boardman* v *Phipps* (1967). Steve may be liable for director's fees as a constructive trustee.

(c) Section 32, TA 1925 (power of advancement) – but it is not her money yet! Is she asking for too much? She is entitled to one-third of £500,000 and only half of this can be advanced.

(d) Section 31, TA 1925 (power of maintenance) – does the gift carry the intermediate income? Even so, is this a proper case for maintenance? Trustees are committed to paying sums for years to come.

 Make your answer stand out

You must know and apply the basic statute law accurately to gain a reasonable mark but for a really good mark you should do some research in the case law, especially on powers of advancement.

READ TO IMPRESS

Cottrell, R. (1971) 'Re Remnant's Settlement Trusts', 34 MLR 98.

Dunn, A. (2001) 'Trusting in the Prudent Woman of Business' in *Feminist Perspectives on Equity and Trusts*, edited by S. Scott-Hunt and H. Lim, London: Cavendish Press.

Francis D. (2008) 'Hastings-Bass and his Scottish friends', 24 SLT 161.

Getzler, J. (2008) 'Excluding Fiduciary Duties: The Problem of Investment Banks', LQR 15.

Koh, J. (2003) 'Once a Director, Always a Fiduciary?', 62 CLJ 403.

Luxton, P. (1997) 'Variations of Trusts: Settlor's Intentions and the Consent Principle in Saunders v. Vautier', 60 MLR 719.

McCormack, C. (1998) 'The Liabilities of Trustees for Gross Negligence', Conv. 100.

Mitchell C. (2006) 'Reining in the Rule in Hastings-Bass', 122 LQR 35.

Nolan R. and Conaglen M. (2006) 'Hastings-Bass and Third Parties', 65 CLJ 499.

NOTES

NOTES

12

Breach of trust

Revision checklist

Essential points you should know:

- [ ] when a breach of trust can arise
- [ ] the distinction between actions *in rem* and actions *in personam*
- [ ] the different principles on which compensation is awarded for breach of trust: significance of *Target Holdings* v *Redfern (a firm)* [1996]
- [ ] when a person who has received trust property in breach of trust can be liable to the beneficiaries
- [ ] when a person who has assisted in a breach of trust (as distinct from receiving trust property) can be liable to the beneficiaries
- [ ] how to apply the rules governing the tracing of trust property
- [ ] the personal liability of trustees

▮ Topic map

What is a breach
of trust?

Remedies of the beneficiary:
Actions *in rem* and actions *in personam* –
what is the difference?

Compensation for breach of trust

Restitution of unauthorised profits

Liability of a person as a constructive
trustee to make restitution of trust property

Personal liability of a person who
has assisted in a breach of trust

Injunction to restrain a breach
of trust

Tracing

At common law

In equity

Personal liability of trustees

A printable version of this topic map is available from **www.pearsoned.co.uk/lawexpress**

Introduction

This is a complex area and needs careful study. The key is understanding how the different remedies interlock.

First learn the basic rules, concentrating on what each remedy is trying to achieve, and completely ignoring the details. When you are clear on this, move on! This way you will find that you are well equipped to answer a problem question and you can then progress to further reading to enable you to tackle an essay question.

Important note: In this chapter we are looking at remedies against either the trustees or the trust property.

ASSESSMENT ADVICE

Essay questions An essay question is likely to focus on the remedies available for a breach of trust. These are the following possibilities:

- a general question, as above
- one on compensation, where you will need a good knowledge of case law, in particular *Target Holdings* v *Redferns (a firm)* [1996]
- a detailed look at tracing remedies: here you may be asked to compare tracing in equity with that at common law or, as below, you may be just asked to look at tracing in equity.

Problem questions A likely question is a detailed one on following trust property where there has been a breach of trust. An example is set out below. Provided you take a logical approach you can earn very good marks here as there is usually a right or wrong answer to most points with some areas having room for discussion so that really good students can earn extra marks. An area to concentrate on when revising!

▌Sample question

Can you answer this question? Below is a typical problem question that could arise on this topic. Guidelines on answering the question are included at the end of the chapter while a sample essay question and guidance on tackling it can be found on the companion website.

PROBLEM QUESTION

Joanna is a trustee of a fund set up by Anne for the benefit of her daughter, Sally. In 2001 Joanna transferred £20,000 from the trust account into her own personal account which, before the transfer, stood at £10,000. She then paid into her personal account the sum of £15,000 which she held as trustee under the will of her friend Dave.

In 2002 she withdrew £12,000 from her account to buy a racehorse but the horse had to be put down when it fell in a race. In 2003 she withdrew a further £6000 which she spent on tickets in a prize draw. She won first prize of £1000. In 2004 she withdrew £25,000 which she spent on a vintage car. In 2005 Joanna withdrew to a monastery in Tibet. She wrote to both Sally and Dave enclosing a cheque for £1000 for each of them and expressing remorse at what she had done. She donated all the rest of the money to the monastery. Joanna gave the car, which is now valued at £7000, to her daughter Millie.

Joanna has now been declared bankrupt.

Advise her trustee in bankruptcy and the beneficiaries under both trusts as to what remedies are available to them to restore the property to the trust.

▌What is a breach of trust?

Trustees are in breach of trust if they fail to observe the duties laid on them by equity and by the trust instrument.

> **REVISION NOTE**
>
> Go back to Chapter 11 and check that you are familiar with the duties of trustees.

Breaches may be:

■ Fraudulent (e.g. wrongly taking trust property). *Attorney-General for Hong Kong* v *Reid* [1994] (see Chapter 9) is a good example of fraud.

■ Negligent (e.g. failing to review investments at proper intervals).

EXAM TIP

Begin your answer to a problem question on remedies by identifying the actual breach of trust which has occurred. Hardly any student does but this is the most important issue: no breach, no remedy, end of question! Of course there will be a breach but find it!

■ Remedies of the beneficiary

Actions *in rem* and actions *in personam*

An action *in personam* may be brought against the trustee for damages for breach of trust, but an action *in rem* may be brought to recover the trust property.

Example 12.1

Action *in personam*

A trustee has a duty to invest the trust property and in this case invests all of the £5m trust fund in a small company on the advice of an inexperienced financial adviser. In fact all of the money is lost when the company goes into liquidation. The beneficiaries are entitled to a remedy but the position is not straightforward as they may not be entitled to all of the money back. It may be that there was a reason for investing some of the money in that company, but not all of it, or it may be that, on the facts, there was no liability at all as the advice was not negligent. Whatever the outcome, the point is that the remedy is for money compensation and is against the trustee personally (*in personam*).

Example 12.2

Action *in rem*

A trustee of money in a bank account in the name of the trust wrongfully withdraws that money and puts it in his own bank account. The beneficiaries have a straightforward remedy: the return of the money. This is a remedy *in rem*, i.e. against the thing itself: in this example, the restitution of the money.

Types of remedies

These are as follows:

(a) compensation for breach of trust, as in Example 12.1
(b) restitution of unauthorised profits
(c) personal liability as a constructive trustee to make restitution of trust property
(d) liability of a person who has assisted in a breach of trust
(e) an injunction to restrain a breach of trust
(f) liability to account as a constructive trustee where there is a right to trace trust property into that person's hands, as in Example 12.2.

It may help to look at the remedies diagrammatically. In Figure 12.1 the letters refer to the list above:

Figure 12.1

Figure 12.1 is deliberately called a snapshot: this topic is complex as it involves a number of different remedies and so at this stage it is only possible to give a general idea of where the remedies fit in. However, it is vital to start in this way.

EXAM TIP

When you are faced with a problem question on remedies draw a diagram like Figure 12.1 so that you are absolutely clear where the different remedies sought in the question fit in.

We will now look at each of the remedies in turn.

(a) Compensation for breach of trust

This remedy is appropriate where there has been, for example, negligence in the exercise of a duty under the trust, such as a duty to invest.

Target Holdings Ltd v *Redferns* (a firm) [1996] 1 AC 421 (HL)

Concerning: principles to be applied when assessing compensation for breach of trust

Facts

X, solicitors, were acting for a mortgagor (borrower) and a mortgagee (lender) and received a mortgage advance on trust to release it to the mortgagor when the transfers of properties were executed. However, in breach of trust they released it early, on the day before contracts were exchanged, and the mortgagee subsequently lost money as the value of the properties had been overstated. The mortgagee claimed against the solicitors for this loss.

Legal principle

In assessing compensation for breach of trust in commercial dealings such as this, bearing in mind that the solicitor was only a bare trustee, a trustee is only liable for losses caused by the breach and not for losses which would have occurred in any event. The mortgage would have gone through anyway, and so the fact that the solicitors had released the mortgage advance early did not cause the loss.

(b) Restitution of unauthorised profits

This remedy is appropriate where there has been a breach of a fiduciary duty by making an unauthorised profit.

REVISION NOTE

Go back to Chapter 9 and check that you know the cases (e.g. *Boardman* v *Phipps* [1967]) on fiduciary duties and their breach.

In *Tang Man Sit* v *Capacious Investments Ltd* [1996] the remedies of compensation and restitution were both possible and the claimant had to choose between them.

(c) Personal liability as a constructive trustee to make restitution of trust property

These are often called knowing receipt cases.

Example 12.3

John is trustee of a small charity. The charity owns a mini-bus and John sells this, in breach of trust, to Jack. The charity wish to take action.

The charity could claim against John under (b) above to make restitution of the money he has received. In addition it could claim against Jack if Jack is a constructive trustee. Will he be? Jack may say that he had no idea that the mini-bus belonged to the charity.

! Don't be tempted to...

Make sure that you can discuss the two current views on the test for liability and apply them to a problem question.

1 Lord Millet in *Twinsectra* v *Yardley* (2002): 'Liability for knowing receipt is receipt based. It does not depend on fault.' The essence of this approach is that it imposes strict liability.
2 Nourse LJ in *Bank of Credit and Commerce International (Overseas) Ltd* v *Akindele* [2001]: 'The recipient's state of knowledge must be such as to make it unconscionable for him to retain the benefit of the receipt.' The essence of this approach is that it does involve fault.

The test of Nourse LJ in *Akindele* is generally thought to represent the current law but this is a CA decision and the Supreme Court will shortly hear an appeal in *Charter Plc* v *City Index Ltd. and others* (2007) which will give an opportunity to review the law. Meanwhile read Gardner (2009) for a clear summary on the present state of play.

✓ Make your answer stand out

Note Gardner's suggestion (reference above) that in addition to liability for knowing receipt as a trustee there could be personal restitutionary liability for unjust enrichment.

See also *Farah Constructions Pty Ltd and others* v *Say-Dee Pty Ltd* (2007) where the High Court of Australia held that liability for receipt of trust property is not based on a general principle of unjust enrichment and rejected the notion that liability was strict and not fault based.

If a person is a volunteer (i.e. has received trust property as a gift) then they must always restore the property.

 Make your answer stand out

The decision in *Farah Constructions* is of great importance and the divergent approaches of the Australian courts are a perfect example of the debate which will always exist in equity. See the excellent analysis of the Court of Appeal's decision by Nolan and Conaglen (2007).

(d) Liability of a person who has assisted in a breach of trust

Example 12.4

Take Example 12.3 above. Suppose that when John wanted to sell the mini-bus he asked Steve, a friend, to find a buyer and it was through Steve that Jack bought it.

Here it is wrong to talk of a person like Steve as a constructive trustee as he has not received trust property but he can be made liable in equity.

Lord Hutton in *Twinsectra* v *Yardley* (2002):

The person must be dishonest and this means that his conduct must be dishonest by the ordinary standards of reasonable and honest people and *he realised* that by those standards his conduct was dishonest. (My italics)

This involves a subjective element (see italicised words above) and this has caused controversy. In *Barlow Clowes International (in liquidation)* v *Eurotrust International Ltd* (2006), the Judicial Committee of the Privy Council held that in cases of dishonest assistance in a breach of trust a person is dishonest if they had knowledge of the elements of the transaction which rendered their participation contrary to the ordinary standards of honest behaviour.

Make your answer stand out

Consider whether the decision in *Barlow Clowes* (above) has changed the law from what it was thought to be after the decision of the House of Lords in *Twinsectra* v *Yardley*. Look at *Abou-Rahmah* v *Abacha* (2006) and especially the judgment of Arden LJ.

(e) Injunction to restrain a breach of trust

REVISION NOTE

Injunctions are dealt with in Chapter 2.

Example 12.5

Suppose that the beneficiaries in Example 12.4 had learned in advance of John's plans to sell the mini-bus. They could have restrained him from doing this by an injunction.

(f) Tracing

KEY DEFINITION: Tracing

The term, as with restitution, is often misunderstood. It is not a remedy as such but a right to trace (i.e. follow) trust property into the hands of a person who then becomes a constructive trustee of it.

Example 12.6

Jane is trustee of the funds at her local tennis club. She takes out £5000 from the funds and uses the money to buy a car. Can the tennis club trace its funds to her car so that the car becomes trust property and, if it wishes, could the club sell it?

Rules on tracing

Tracing at common law

This right is limited and it does not allow **tracing** in one of the most common cases: where the defendant has mixed the trust's money in his own bank account and then gone bankrupt.

Tracing in equity

Keep two distinct points in mind:

1 Is tracing possible?
2 If so, can it be done?

First, there are four conditions as to whether tracing is possible:

1 Existence of a fiduciary relationship.

 Make your answer stand out

The necessity for this has been criticised. Lord Millett in *Foskett* v *McKeown* [2001] said that there was no logical justification for it.

2 Existence of an equitable proprietary interest (e.g. that of a beneficiary).
3 Tracing would not be inequitable: see *Re Diplock* [1948].
4 Property must be in a traceable form. This means that the property must be ascertainable and this will not be so if, for example, it has been spent on a holiday.

KEY CASE

Bishopsgate Investment Management (in liquidation) v *Homan* [1995] Ch 211 (CA)

Concerning: loss of the right to trace

Facts

The facts of this case do not aid an understanding of the legal principle.

Legal principle

Tracing will not be permitted into an overdrawn account as clearly the property into which it is sought to trace has disappeared.

Second, we turn to consider whether tracing can be done.

Rules on tracing in equity

Follow through these rules. They are the ones most likely to arise in an exam.

EXAM TIP

Problem questions will almost certainly concentrate on the position where a trustee has mixed trust money with his own.

KEY CASE

Re Hallett's Estate (1880) 13 Ch D 696 (HC)

Concerning: withdrawals from an account

Facts

The facts of this case do not aid an understanding of the legal principle.

Legal principle

When making withdrawals from an account a trustee is presumed to spend his own money first. Once the amount in the account falls below the amount of trust funds then it is assumed that part of the trust funds must have been spent. Any later payments into the account are not treated as repayments of the trust money unless the trustee has shown an intention to do this (*Roscoe (James) (Bolton)* v *Winder* [1915]).

Example 12.7

A trustee (X) puts £10,000 of trust money and £3000 of his own money into the trust account. He takes out £11,000 and spends it. £3000 of this is presumed to be his own money, but the remainder must be trust money. Therefore there is now £2000 of trust money left. He then puts £3000 into the account. This is presumed to be his own money unless X shows an intention to repay the trust money. If he does not then although the beneficiaries can claim the £2000 in the account they will have to take their place along with X's other creditors in a claim for the balance.

Rule two

In *Re Oatway* [1903] it was held that if a trustee mixes his own and trust money in an account and then takes all the money and spends it on identifiable property the beneficiaries have a first charge on this property for the recovery of the trust money.

KEY CASE

Foskett v *McKeown* [2001] 1 AC 102 (HL)

Concerning: position where the trust fund has increased in value

Facts

The facts of this case do not aid an understanding of the legal principle.

Legal principle

Lord Millett held that the beneficiary may claim either:

(a) a share in the fund in proportion to which the original trust fund bore to the mixed fund at the date when it was mixed, or

(b) they may have a lien on the fund to secure a personal claim against the fund for the return of the money (per Lord Millett).

Thus any increase in value can be claimed under option (a) but if the fund has decreased in value, then the beneficiaries can have a lien under option (b) for the amount that they are owed.

Rule three

The position where mixed funds in an account represent the funds of two or more trusts or the funds of a trust and an innocent volunteer. We are concerned here with two types of competing claim:

1 between two or more persons with a right to trace
2 between a person with a right to trace and an innocent volunteer.

Rule in *Re Clayton* (1816)

The rule in this case provides that in the case of an active continuing bank account the trustee is regarded as having taken out of the fund whatever had been first put in: basically, 'first in, first out'.

Example 12.8

X, a trustee, puts £1000 of trust A money into a bank account on 1 June and £500 of trust B money into the same account on 2 June. There is now a total of £1500 trust money in the account. X then takes out £1200, and, in breach of trust, spends this. As the trust A money was put in first he is presumed to have taken all of this out together with £200 of trust B money. The remaining £300 belongs to trust B.

In *Barlow Clowes International Ltd (in liquidation)* v *Vaughan* [1992] the rule in *Re Clayton* (1816) – *Clayton's Case* – was not applied to claims by investors regarding share in the assets of a company which had managed investment plans for them. The exact date on which sums owing to individuals were paid in could have simply been by chance (e.g. delay in delivery of their letter with the money).

■ Personal liability of trustees and beneficiaries

Note that:

■ Trustees can escape liability: note carefully s. 61 and s. 62 of the Trustee Act 1925 and also the general equitable principle.

■ Where a beneficiary participates in, or consents to, a breach of trust then the court may impound his/her interest so that it is available to replace any loss to the trust and so can be used to satisfy the claims of other beneficiaires who have suffered loss.

■ A beneficiary who is of full age and capacity and who is in possession of all the relevant facts and freely consents to a breach of trust cannot sue in respect of it afterwards.

EXAM TIP

The above points may arise in a question involving trustees. See Chapter 11.

■ Chapter summary: putting it all together

Test yourself

☐ Can you tick all the points from the **revision checklist** at the beginning of this chapter?

☐ Attempt the **sample question** from the beginning of this chapter using the answer guidelines below.

☐ Go to the **companion website** to access more revision support online, including interactive quizzes, sample questions with answer guidelines, 'you be the marker' exercises, flashcards and podcasts you can download.

Answer guidelines

See the problem question at the start of the chapter.

Approaching the question

Joanna is a trustee and has committed breaches of trust. Therefore equitable remedies are available against her. Of these, the personal remedies are of no use as she is bankrupt and so has no assets. So we must turn to remedies against the trust property – proprietary remedies and, in particular, tracing. Go through the conditions which must be satisfied for tracing remedy to exist – there is an equitable proprietary interest but two conditions may not be satisfied in each case: tracing must not be inequitable and the property must be in traceable form. If a condition does not exist then there is no point in considering tracing further.

Important points to include

Follow through the sequence of events:

1 Joanna deposits £20,000 from the first trust account (we will refer to this as Trust A) into her own account. Her account then stands at £30,000.
2 She then pays in £15,000 from Trust B. Her account now stands at £45,000.
3 She withdraws £12,000 from her account to buy a racehorse. This must come first from her own money (*Re Hallett's Estate* (1880)) which is now spent and then probably from Trust A money (*Clayton's Case* (1816) but note here *Barlow Clowes International Ltd* v *Vaughan* (1992)). As the racehorse is dead the money is no longer traceable. So there is now £33,000 left in the account made up of:
    ■ £18,000 Trust A money (£20,000 less £2000 spent in breach of trust)
    ■ £15,000 Trust B money.
4 Withdrawal of £6000 to buy tickets: from Trust A. The prize of £1000 may be claimed by Trust A (*Re Oatway* [1903], this sum has not been included in the final calculation, *Re Tilley's Will Trust* [1967] and *Foskett* v *McKeown* [2001]). There is now £27,000 of which £12,000 is left.
5 Withdrawal of £25,000 to buy a car: this must be first from Trust A (£12,000). Trust A is now exhausted. And then £13,000 from Trust B. Now £2000 is left of Trust B's money.
6 Loss of £18,000 on the car: Trusts A and B will share rateably in any losses.
7 Money to monastery: must come from Trust B – cannot be traced? Is tracing inequitable? *Re Diplock* [1948].
8 Letter: appears to be repayment – *Roscoe* v *Winder* [1915].

▶

Make your answer stand out

Many students omit the material in the introductory paragraph. This is vital. Do include it!

READ TO IMPRESS

Gardner, (2003) *An Introduction to the Law of Trusts*, 2nd edn, Oxford: Oxford University Press, pp. 265–85.

Gardner (2009) 'Moment of Truth for Knowing Receipt?', 125 LQR 30.

Nolan, R. and Conaglen, M. (2007) 'Strict Liability for Receipt of Misapplied Trust Property – Confusion Abounds', at 66 CLJ 19.

NOTES

And finally, before the exam . . .

Test yourself

- [ ] Look at the **revision checklists** at the start of each chapter. Are you happy that you can now tick them all? If not, go back to the particular chapter and work through the material again. If you are still struggling, seek help from your tutor.
- [ ] Go to the **companion website** and revisit the online resources.
  - [ ] Take the full **study plan** test to assess your knowledge in all areas.
  - [ ] Try the **practice quizzes** and see if you can score full marks for each chapter.
  - [ ] Attempt to answer the **sample questions** for each chapter within the time limit.
  - [ ] Use the **flashcards** to test your recall of the legal principles of the cases and statutes you've revised and the definitions of important terms.
  - [ ] See if you can spot the strengths and weaknesses of the sample answers in **'you be the marker'**.
  - [ ] Listen to the **podcast** and then attempt the question it discusses.
- [ ] Go through each case in the text and make sure that you know the legal principle of each. You may find it helpful to make a separate list of these cases, write down the name of each and under it leave space for you to write in the legal principle. Do the same for statutes. Concentrate on the legal principle and remember to use the facts to illustrate the principle.

☐ Do the same for all the key definitions.

☐ Identify some of the key concepts of equity: a good start would be notice, discretion in the award of remedies, fiduciaries and unconscionability. Make sure that you can discuss them as concepts rather then just using them as terms.

☐ Check through all areas where there is an overlap between topics because this will help you in revising. This is dealt with below.

Linking it all up

Check where there are overlaps between subject areas. (You may want to review the 'revision note' boxes throughout this book.) Make a careful note of these as knowing how one topic may lead into another can increase your marks significantly. Here are some examples:

✓ Constructive trusts. A question on the nature of equity, nature of trusts, trustees, the fiduciary relationship, trusts of the home and, of course, a question on this topic itself.

✓ Trustees. A question on constructive trusts, the fiduciary relationship and a question on this topic itself.

✓ Three certainties. A question on secret trusts, formalities, constitution and one on the three certainties itself.

✓ Non-charitable purpose trusts. A question on the nature of trusts, charitable trusts (problem questions often ask you about situations involving both charitable and non-charitable trusts), the nature of equity and this topic itself.

✓ Equitable maxims. Essay questions on the maxims are excellent vehicles for bringing together knowledge on various topics: e.g. equity does not allow a statute to be used as an instrument of fraud: secret trusts, constructive trusts. Equity looks to the intent and not the form: secret trusts, constitution of trusts, certainty of intention. Equity does not assist a volunteer. Constitution of trusts. Nature of a trust.

✓ Nature of equity. This topic is such a good example and such a common exam question that a more detailed plan for bringing together different strands of the whole subject is set out below.

■ Sample question

Below is an essay question that incorporates overlapping areas of the law. See if you can answer this question drawing upon your knowledge of the whole subject area. Guidelines on answering this question are included at the end of this section.

> ## ESSAY QUESTION
>
> 'The function of the common law is to establish rules to govern the generality of cases ... The function of equity is to restrain or restrict the exercise of legal rights and powers in particular cases, whenever it would be unconscionable for them to be exercised to the full.'
>
> Watt, *Trusts and Equity* (2003)
>
> Consider and illustrate this statement by reference to the nature and application of modern equity.

Answer guidelines

Approaching the question

The question asks about modern equity so no marks at all for history! Do look through the whole of this book and choose points which you can use to illustrate this answer. For example, you could choose material in Chapter 1 on the nature of equity and Chapter 9 on constructive trusts, but make your own choice!

Important points to include

■ Deal with the common law point: is it true to say that it is only concerned with generalities? Generally yes. For example, consideration in contract applies across the whole range of contracts, but with the duty of care in negligence there are variations. No need for much detail on common law but show you can contrast the two systems.

■ Contrast equity and deal with the exact points raised.

■ There are two of these:

   (a) Does equity operate to restrict or restrain legal rights and responsibilities?
   (b) Is the basis of its jurisdiction unconscionability?

▶

In both cases it can be suggested that the statement oversimplifies:

(a) Equity is not just about seeking to prevent injustice occurring in the application of legal rules.
(b) Equitable jurisdiction is not just about restraining unconscionability.

Now back up these points with specific examples chosen from chapters in this book. Your choice! But do make sure that you tie your points together in a theme related to (a) and (b) above. An answer which reads like (and is!) a collection of disjointed points will get a very poor mark. A useful tip is to make the first sentence of one paragraph follow on from the last sentence of the preceding one.

 Make your answer stand out

A clear analysis of terminology is needed. For instance, what is meant by 'unconscionability' and 'principle'? Look at the '*Read to impress*' section at the end of Chapter 1 for sources.

NOTES

Glossary of terms

The glossary is divided into two parts: *key definitions* and *other useful terms*. The key definitions can be found within the chapter in which they occur, as well as here, below. These definitions are the essential terms that you must know and understand in order to prepare for an exam. The additional list of terms provides further definitions of useful terms and phrases which will also help you answer examination and coursework questions effectively. These terms are highlighted in the text as they occur but the definition can only be found here.

Key definitions

Advancement	Payment of capital to beneficiaries before they are entitled.
Bare trustee	A trustee with no active duties and so can be given directions by the beneficiary to transfer the legal estate.
Beneficiaries	Those for whom the property is held in trust.
Constitution of a trust	A trust is constituted when the legal title to the trust property is vested in the trustee(s).
Constructive trusts	Defined by Millett (Equity's Place in the Law of Commerce 1998 114 LQR 214) as arising 'whenever the circumstances are such that it would be unconscionable for the owner of the legal title to assert his own beneficial interest and deny the beneficial interest of another'.
Cy-près	So near (i.e. allows property to be used for charitable purposes so near to the original ones where these have failed).
Discretionary trust	Where the trustees have a discretion as to whether a person will be a beneficiary or not.
Estoppel	This arises when the representee has been led to act on the representation of the representor. If the representee

	then acts to their detriment on the basis of this promise, then in equity the court may grant them a remedy.
Fixed trusts	Where the interests in the trust property are fixed in the trust instrument.
Half-secret trusts	Where the will or other document discloses the existence of the trusts but not the details.
Injunction	An order requiring a party either to do or not to do a particular act.
Maintenance	Means payment of income to beneficiaries before they are entitled.
Marriage consideration	In equity this includes the husband and wife and the issue of the marriage.
Misrepresentation	An untrue statement of fact which induces a person to enter into a transaction.
Notice	A purchaser is taken to have notice of an equitable interest unless they had either actual notice of the equitable interest of the beneficiaries, or constructive notice or imputed notice.
Protective trusts	Where there is a determinable life interest (determinable e.g. on the bankruptcy of the beneficiary) followed by a discretionary trust if the interest does determine.
Rectification	Where a written instrument (e.g. a contract) does not accord with the actual intentions of the parties it can be made to do so by an order of rectification.
Rescission	This remedy restores the parties to their position before the contract or other transaction was made.
Resulting trust	The beneficial interest results to, or jumps back to, the settlor who created the trust. The basis of an action founded on a resulting trust is therefore that one is seeking to recover one's own property.
Rule against perpetuities	Section 5 of the Perpetuities and Accumulations Act 2009 (which comes into force on a date to be appointed in 2010) provides for a perpetuity period of 125 years.
Rule for certainty of objects in discretionary trusts	'Can it be said with certainty that any given individual is or is not a member of the class?'
Rule for certainty of objects in fixed trusts	All the beneficiaries must be capable of being listed, i.e. there must be no doubt as to who the beneficiaries are.

Secret trusts	Where the will or other document does not disclose the existence of the trust.
Settlor	The settlor is in effect the creator of the trust which is created by the settlor transferring property to the trustees to hold on trust or alternatively declaring that they are the trustees. If the trust is created by will then the trust is created by the testator.
Specific performance (SP)	An order requiring the performance of obligations under a contract. Whereas injunctions are generally negative (you must not), SP is positive (you must).
Tracing	A right to trace (i.e. follow) trust property into the hands of a person who then becomes a constructive trustee of it.
Trust	'A trust is a relationship which arises when property is vested in a person (or persons) called the trustees, which those trustees are obliged to hold for the benefit of other persons called the *cestuis que trust* or beneficiaries' (Hanbury and Martin, *Modern Equity*, 18th edn, p. 49).
Trust is unconstituted	A trust is unconstituted when the legal title to the trust property is not vested in the trustees.
Volunteer	A person who has not provided any consideration for a promise.

■ Other useful terms

Administrator	Person(s) appointed by the court to administer the estate of a person who has died intestate.
Bona vacantia	Vacant goods, so ownership goes to the Crown.
Executor	Person(s) nominated to act in a fiduciary capacity in the carrying out of a testator's will.
Grant of probate	Authorises an executor(s) to deal with the estate.
Inter vivos	Between the living.
Intestate	Where a person dies without leaving a valid will.
Will	Written document duly executed, setting out the manner in which the testator's property is to be distributed on his/her death. (Note: it is possible to have a valid oral will in the cases of those serving in the armed forces in time of war and those serving at sea.)

Index

Emboldened entries refer to those appearing in the glossary

acceptance of trust 107, 108, 115
acquiescence of trust 108
administration of equity 9
administrator 96, 209
advancement, powers of 173, 179–80, 184, 207
  see also presumption
animals, trusts to care for 54–5
appointment of trustees 175
Attorney General 152
Australia 11, 194–5
automatic theory 128

bad faith 176
bare trustee 59, 73–4, 76, 193, 207
beneficial interests 79, 122, 182
  failure to dispose of 125
  in the home 123
beneficiaries 8–9, 207
  compelling constitution 92–4
  contract to transfer equitable interest 75–6
  declare themselves trustees 76
  disclaim equitable interest 77
  surrender equitable interest 77
  under staff pension funds appoint nominees to receive benefits from funds 78
beneficiary principle and purpose trusts 49–62, 127
  exceptions to beneficiary principle 54–5
  future development of the law 60
  non-charitable purpose trusts 52–4
  ways in which beneficiary priciple comes into conflict with other rules and concepts:
  perpetuity rules, effect of 56–7
  unincorporated associations, gifts to 57–60

ways in which beneficiary principle comes into conflict with other rules and concepts 55–60
bona vacantia 166, 209
bonus notice 144
breach of confidence 17
breach of trust 133, 187–202
  definition 190–1
  fraudulent 190
  personal liability of trustees and beneficiaries 200
  tracing 196–200
  see also remedies of beneficiary
bribes, receipt of 138

Canada 123
certainties 33–47, 85, 204
  conceptual and evidential 43
  effect of lack of certainty 43–4
  fixed trusts 41–3
  of intention 36–9, 47, 80, 103, 105, 107, 204
  of objects (ie beneficiaries) 35, 41, 42, 43, 45, 47, 152
  beneficiary principle and purpose trusts 51
  secret and half-secret trusts 107, 115
  perpetuities, rule against and discretionary trusts 46
  power to cure uncertainty 44
  of subject matter 35, 39–41, 47, 107
cestuis que trust *see* beneficiaries
characteristics of equity 5
charitable trusts 53, 149–68, 204
  advantages of charitable status 152–3
  charitable or benevolent objects 162–3
  charitable purposes recognised by law 154–8
  education, advancement of 155–6
  heads of charity 157–8

poverty, prevention or relief of 155
religion, advancement of 156–7
definition of charity 154
failure of charitable and non-charitable gifts 125, 163–6
forms of charitable organisations 154
must be exclusively charitable 162–3
perpetuity, rule against 153
public benefit, recognised, requirement of 158–62
Charity Commission 152, 157, 158, 159–60, 161, 162
codicil 110
coercion, actual 27
common law 3, 9, 10, 12, 94, 189, 205
damages 18, 93
promises made in a deed 92
remedy 6
tracing 196
communication 114–15
of intention to create a trust 107–8, 112
rules 108
valid 115
compensation for breach of trust 189, 192–3
condition precedent 35
conflict of interest 184
conscience 4, 12
consideration 88
in contract 205
in equity 92
constitution of a trust 38, 69, 83–98, 204, 207
beneficiaries compelling constitution 92–4
indirect 95–7
methods of constituting a trust 88–92
declaration of settlor as trustee 88–90
settlor does all in power to constitute trust 91–2
transfer to others as trustees 90
trustees' position where trust is incompletely constituted 94
ways in which a trust can be constituted 86–8
constructive trusts 12, 127, 204, 205, 207
breach of trust 192, 193–5
certainties 38
constitution 97

formalities 69, 70, 75
secret and half-secret trusts 113
trusteeship 173, 175, 184
see also constructive trusts and estoppel
constructive trusts and estoppel 131–45
bribes, receipt of 138
definition of constructive trusts 134–7
home, trusts of 139–41
institutional trusts 133, 141–2
promissory estoppel 142
proprietary estoppel 142–4
remedial trusts 31, 133, 140, 141–2, 144
statute as an instrument of fraud 138–9
contracts 3, 24–5, 205
contractual licences 141
Court of Appeal 9
Court of Chancery 5
covenant, deed of 92
Crown 166
cy-près doctrine 163, 164, 165, 166, 207

damages 18, 20, 23, 93, 142, 191
declaration of self as trustee 89
declaration of settlor as trustee 88–90
declaration of trust 70, 76, 80, 126
declaration of a trust of land 68–70
declaration of trust would need to be in writing 90
definition of equity 4–6
definition of a trust 8
delegation by trustees 173, 181
detrimental reliance 139
development of the trust 8–9
direction to beneficiary to trustees that they are not to hold on trust for another person 72–3
discretion 6, 176, 204
discretionary equitable remedy 18, 31
discretionary trust 35, 42–3, 45, 46, 47, 207
disposal of surplus funds of unincorporated associations, law on 57
disposition 76
donatio mortis causa (DMC) 96–7, 98, 133
duties of trustees 173, 174, 183, 190
see also under trusteeship
duty of care 183

in negligence 205
duty, fiduciary 12, 193

education, advancement of 155–6, 157, 159, 160, 167
employment, contract of 25
enforcer 60
equitable interests 122
equitable interests, dispositions of, arising under trusts 70–8
  application of s.53(1)(c) 71–2
  beneficiary contracts to transfer equitable interest 75–6
  beneficiary declares himself trustee 76
  beneficiary disclaims equitable interest 77
  beneficiary surrenders equitable interest 77
  beneficiary under staff pension fund appoints nominee to receive benefits from fund 78
  direction to beneficiary to trustees that they are not to hold on trust for another person 72–3
  failure to comply with requirements of s.53(1)(c) 78
  new trusts are declared by trustee within consent of beneficiary 74–5
  transfer by beneficiary of equitable interest to another 72
  transfer of legal estate by bare trustee to another 73–4
equitable interests need to be in writing 92
equitable lease 10
equitable maxims *see* equity
equitable principles 142
equitable proprietary interest 197, 201
equitable remedies and doctrines 5–6, 15–31, 93, 141, 201
  characteristics 18
  rectification 25–6, 208
  rescission 25, 208
  undue influence 17, 26–30, 123
  see also injunctions; specific performance
'equity does not assist a person with unclean hands' maxim 7, 123

'equity looks to the intent rather than the form' maxim 103, 204
equity may assist a volunteer 95–7
'equity will not allow a statute to be used as an engine of fraud' maxim 103, 106, 204
'equity will not assist a volunteer' maxim 85, 87–8, 92, 93, 95, 195, 204
estoppel 97, 98, 139, 207–8
  see also constructive trusts and estoppel
exclusively equitable 18
executor 36, 68, 209
express acceptance of trust 108
express trusts 38, 69, 70, 113, 115, 127
  formal 120
  functional 120
  and resulting constructive trusts, differences between 120–1
  substantive 120

fee charging 160
fiduciaries 183
  trustees as 175–6
fiduciary duty 12
  breach of 193
fiduciary principle 133, 173
fiduciary relationship 135–7, 138, 141, 145, 182, 197, 204
fixed trusts 35, 42, 208
formalities 65–80, 85, 86, 204
  declaration of a trust of land 68–70
  necessity for 78–9
  see also equitable interests, dispositions of, arising under trusts
fourth head 159
fraud 69–70, 78, 106, 124
freezing order (*Mareva*) 7, 17, 21, 22

general equitable principle 200
gifts 46, 91, 107, 111
  absolute 39, 47
  by will 106
  deeds of 92
  incomplete 97
  incomplete, perfecting 95
  inter vivos 35, 106, 209

non-charitable 164, 166
    to unincorporated associations 51, 55,
        57–60
grant of probate 209

half-secret trusts 208
    see also secret and half-secret trusts
hardship amounting to injustice 5–6, 18
High Court 9
home, trusts of 12, 135, 139–41, 204

impartiality, duty of 177
implied trust 69
imposition of a trust 37, 47
imputed trusts 120
in personam 18, 191
in rem 191
information, duty to give 177
informed consent 137
injunctions 7, 19–23, 142, 192, 208
    interlocutory 19–22
    permanent 20
    perpetual 19
    quia timet 19, 20
    to restrain a breach of trust 196
intention 114, 115
    common 121, 128
    lack of 128
    presumed 121–2
    rationale 106
    to create a trust 89, 92, 107, 109
    to make an immediate gift or release a debt
        96
    see also under certainties
inter vivos declarations of trusts 69, 209
inter vivos gift 35, 106, 209
intestate 96, 209
investment, powers of 173, 183

joint tenants 111

knowing receipt cases 193–5

land, power to buy 170
land, trust of 68–70
Law Commission 79

legal interest 122
legal rights 205
liability:
    exclusion 181–2
    of person who has assisted in breach of
        trust 195–6
    see also personal liability

maintenance 173, 179–80, 184, 208
'manifested and proved' 68
Mareva order *see* freezing order
marriage consideration 92, 93, 208
maxims *see* equity
misrepresentation 30, 208
modern equity 4, 6, 11, 205

nature of equity and trusts 1–12, 204, 205
    development of the trust 8–9
    Judicature Acts 1873 and 1875 and fusion
        9–10
    maxims of equity 7
    meaning of equity 4–6
    modern equity – developments since 1875 11
negligence, duty of care 205
new trusts are declared by trustee within
        consent of beneficiary 74–5
New Zealand 141
non-charitable gifts, failure of 166
non-charitable purpose trusts 51, 52–4, 56,
        61, 204
non-charitable trusts 151, 152
    failure of 125
non-charitable unincorporated associations 60
notice 9, 204, 208
    actual 9
    constructive 9
    imputed 9

objects *see under* certainties
obligation 105
outside (*dehors*) the will 112

perpetuity *see* rule against perpetuity
personal liability 192
    as constructive trustee to make restitution
        of trust property 193–5

of trustees and beneficiaries 200, 283
personal services, contract for 24–5
political trusts 161–2
poverty, prevention or relief of 155, 157, 159, 160, 167
powers of trustees *see under* trusteeship
precatory words 37, 38
presumption of advancement 121–2, 123–4
principle 206
private trusts 51, 53, 151, 152
   valid 163
profits, unauthorised, restitution of 193
promises made in a deed 92
proprietary interest 177
proprietary remedies 201
protective trusts 208
public benefit 151, 158–62, 164, 167
purchase in the name of another 123
purpose trusts 56
   non-charitable 51, 52–4, 56, 61, 163, 204
   see also beneficiary principle and purpose trusts
put on inquiry 28–9

quia timet injunction 19, 20
Quistclose principle 60, 126, 127

Re Astor principle *see* beneficiary principle
recreational facilities 158
rectification 25–6, 208
relationship of trust 27
religion, advancement of 156–7, 159, 160, 161, 167
remedies 20, 31, 142, 189, 204
   proprietary 201
   see also damages; equitable remedies and doctrines
remedies of beneficiary 191–200
   actions *in rem* and actions *in personam* 191
   compensation for breach of trust 192–3
   injunction to restrain a breach of trust 196
   liability of person who has assisted in breach of trust 195–6
   personal liability as constructive trustee to make restitution of trust property 193–5

restitution of unauthorised profits 193
   tracing 196
removal of trustees 175
rescission 25, 208
restitution 192, 193–5
resulting trusts 117–28, 139, 140, 163, 166, 208
   automatic 122
   basis of 121
   certainties 38, 43, 47
   express trusts and resulting and constructive trusts 120–1
   failure to dispose of beneficial interest 125
   formalities 69, 70
   presumption of advancement 123–4
   purchase in the name of another 123
   secret and half-secret trusts 108, 110, 115
   security for loans, trusts as 125–7
   theories to explain basis of 121–2
retirement of trustees 175
right of beneficiary under trust 18
right to remuneration 174
rule against perpetuities 46, 51, 55, 56–7, 60, 61–2, 153, 208
rule for certainty of objects in discretionary trusts 208
rule for certainty of objects in fixed trusts 208

'safe in the knowledge' 47
Scottish law 177
search orders (*Anton Piller*) 7, 17, 21–2
secret and half-secret trusts 12, 101–16, 120, 133, 204, 208, 209
   acceptance of trust 108
   communication of intention 107–8, 109–10
   distinction between 105
   express or constructive trusts 113
   fraud rationale 106
   intention rationale 106
   intention, subject matter and objects 107
   position where trust is communicated to only one of two or more trustees 111–12
security for loans, trusts as 125–7
settlor 8, 68, 71–2, 91–2, 209

severance 111
signature of settlor 68
silence 108
specific monuments, trusts for upkeep of
    54–5
specific performance 5–6, 7, 17, 22–5, 75,
    93, 94, 209
stamp duty 71–2
statute as an instrument of fraud 138–9
statutory duties 173, 178–9
subject matter *see under* certainties
subsequent failure 165
substantive trusts 141
Supreme Court 9
surety 28–9

tenants in common 111
theft, law of 38
third parties:
    and uncertainty 44
    and undue influence 28–9
tort 3
tracing 192, 196–200, 201, 209
    at common law 196
    in equity 197
    remedies 189
    rules on tracing equity 197–200
transfer by beneficiary of equitable interest to
    another 72
transfer of legal estate by bare trustee to
    another 73–4
trust 209
trust is unconstituted 209
trustees 8, 204
    position where trust is incompletely
        constituted 94
trusteeship 171–84
    appointment of trustees 175
    duties and powers of trustees 176–81
        advancement, powers of 179–80
        delegation by trustees 181
        duty to give information 177

impartiality, duty of 177
land, power to buy 170
maintenance, powers of 179–80
relationship between powers in trust
    instrument and statutory powers
    177
statutory duty of care 178–9
fiduciaries, trustees as 175–6
liability, exclusion of 181–2
powers of trustees 173, 174, 183
retirement and removal of trustees 175
variation of trust by the court 182–3
variation of trust by trustees and
    beneficiaries 182

uncertainty 141
    about a particular fact 44
    conceptual 47
    evidential 47
    power to cure 44
unconscionability 4, 6, 11, 91, 143, 204, 205,
    206
unconstituted trust 87
undue influence 17, 26–30, 123
unenforceability 69
unincorporated associations 62, 165
    gifts to 51, 55, 57–60
    non-charitable 60
unjust enrichment 144, 194

validity of gift 151
validity of a secret and half-secret trust 103
variation of trust by the court 182–3
variation of trust by trustees and beneficiaries
    182
void 69
volunteer 7, 209

'wait and see' provisions 56, 61
'width of the field' 43–4
wills 26, 35, 36, 37, 209